Gandhi's Philosophy of Education

Gandhi's Philosophy
of Education

Glyn Richards

OXFORD
UNIVERSITY PRESS

OXFORD

UNIVERSITY PRESS

YMCA Library Building, Jai Singh Road, New Delhi 110001

Oxford University Press is a department of the University of Oxford.
It furthers the University's objective of excellence in research, scholarship
and education by publishing worldwide in

Oxford   New York

Athens   Auckland   Bangkok   Bogotá   Buenos Aires   Cape Town
Chennai   Dar es Salaam   Delhi   Florence   Hong Kong   Istanbul   Karachi
Kolkata   Kuala Lumpur   Madrid   Melbourne   Mexico City   Mumbai   Nairobi
Paris   São Paulo   Shanghai   Singapore   Taipei   Tokyo   Toronto   Warsaw

with associated companies in Berlin Ibadan

Published in India
by Oxford University Press

ISBN 019 565 2835

Typeset in Goudy
by Eleven Arts, Keshav Puram, Delhi-110035
Printed in India by Rashtriya Printers, Delhi 110032
and published by Manzar Khan, Oxford University Press
YMCA Library Building, Jai Singh Road, New Delhi 110001

For my grandchildren

Preface

My interest in the subject matter of this book was aroused in the first instance when I was writing *The Philosophy of Gandhi*, which contains a chapter on education. In one sense what is contained in the pages that follow is an extension of what is to be found in that chapter: in another sense it goes far beyond it, introducing as it does comparisons with other Hindu reformers, and with Western educationists and philosophers. I am aware that other scholars have shown an interest in this intriguing area of study, and that they may well be continuing their researches in the field. The study I am engaged in here is the result of a period of reflection over the years, though interrupted by some unfortunate and unexpected events. It is in no way an exhaustive treatment of the subject, and should it encourage further researches by inviting comparisons with other educationists, or by prompting further comments on the aim and purpose of education, then it will have served a useful purpose.

My main aim in this study is to indicate the *avant garde* nature of Gandhi's philosophy of education, and to show how modern in some respects his views are despite his initial reluctance to express them. This is particularly true of his pluralistic approach to religious studies, and of the integral relationship he conceives to exist between language and self-identity. It is true also of his views on adult education; on the need for institutions of learning to be self-supporting; on the importance of creativity in the physical as well as the mental spheres; on the significance of music; and on the need for the cultivation of the spirit. Comparisons are drawn with philosophers who have distinctive theories of education, and with educationists who have proposed innovative methods of teaching, in order to illuminate further his views on the subject.

I am indebted to my colleagues for their help and support: to Professors Ninian Smart, Dewi Z. Phillips, and Sir Stewart R. Sutherland for providing me with books they had in their possession; to Professor Herbert Wilson for seeking to acquire books on my behalf; to Professor Cyril G. Williams for his comments; and to the Reverend Ifor Rees for providing me with a copy of one of Whitehead's works. Above all I am grateful for the memory of Helga, who continues to be a source of inspiration.

Glyn Richards
Dunblane, Scotland, and Cardiff, Wales

Contents

Contents

chapter one

True Education

To understand Gandhi's thinking on education, or any other aspect of his philosophy, it is necessary to be aware of what he means by Truth. It is not insignificant that he gave his autobiography the subtitle *The Story of My Experiments with Truth*, and I have endeavoured to show in an earlier work,[1] that his whole life might be regarded as an attempt to live in accordance with Truth. His followers, like Morarji Desai and Acharya Kripalani for instance, are no doubt right in maintaining that he was essentially a practical man, with little or no interest in philosophical or metaphysical speculation as such. My discussions with the former, who was at the time Prime Minister of India, and with the latter, who was one of Gandhi's most ardent disciples, were sufficiently comprehensive to convince me of the accuracy of their judgement. Yet, while it may well have been the case that Gandhi was a man with a practical bent of mind who could not quite be described as a philosopher in the traditional sense of the term, there can be little doubt that his thoughts and actions sprang from firmly held religious and metaphysical beliefs. The nature of those beliefs become evident when we examine what he means by Truth.

It is true to say that it would be wrong to suggest he arrives at the meaning of Truth as a result of a process of philosophical speculation undertaken in the abstract as it were. He is not a speculative philosopher, or a neutral observer, who first seeks to define Truth and then applies it to different aspects of life: rather he is one who is a participant in the Hindu way of life, and who comes to understand what Truth is from the connotation the term has in that form of life.

From his speeches and writings we can discern quite clearly that he equates Truth (*Satya*) with Reality (*Sat*). He asserts unequivocally for instance that for him nothing exists except Truth since Truth is Reality.[2] In true *Advaitin* fashion he asserts that where Truth is, there also is Reality, Knowledge and Bliss, or *Saccidānanda*, which is one of the Upanishadic terms for *Brahman*.[3] So for him Truth is Being itself, or Ultimate Reality, and it is significant that the western theologian Paul Tillich also refers to God as Ultimate Concern, and the Ground of Being. This is an indication of the comparison that can be drawn between the two thinkers, and it is possible because they share a similar form of philosophical idealism.[4] Gandhi, for example, is well aware that when *Brahman* assumes shape or form in order to meet specific human needs for concrete, tangible symbols, it is referred to as *Iśvara*. Tillich for his part refers to God as a symbol for the God beyond God, or the Ground of Being, or Ultimate Concern. What we can conclude from this is that both recognize the need of symbols to represent the Ultimate. For Tillich the personal God is a symbol for the Ground of Being. Gandhi, on the other hand, acknowledges that *Iśvara* is a symbol for *Brahman*, and that while the formless concept of Truth might be sufficient for some people, it has to assume personal form for those who need tangible representations of the Ultimate, and who feel the need of a personal presence.[5] His own preference is for the formless concept of Truth, but he does not consider those devotees who desire tangible symbols, or a more personal concept of God, to be in any way inferior in spirituality or understanding to those who are drawn to the formless concept of the Ultimate.[6]

In accordance with the teaching of *Advaita Vedānta*, Gandhi is able to maintain also that no hard-and-fast distinction can be drawn between the Self within, or the *Ātman*, and Truth (*Satya*). His reference to the soul (*Ātman*), and God (*Brahman*), as knowers rather than objects of knowledge, and his claim that it is not possible for mortal beings to know the Knower of Knowing, bears this out.[7] It is also consistent with the teaching of the Upanishads concerning the identity of *Ātman-Brahman*, a position Gandhi assumes when he maintains that the Self within is at one with the essence of the universe. For him, the whole purpose of life, and the aim of true education, is to know the Self, which is akin to knowing the Truth, and realizing God. The Self or *Ātman*, released from the empirical bonds of darkness and ignorance, or the 'shades of the prison-house' as Wordsworth would describe it,[8] is at one with God, and identical with Truth. Hence his claim that Self-realization is Truth-realization, which in turn is the realization of God. The basic presupposition here is that the existential quest for Truth is akin to seeking to know the true nature of the Self. This in turn involves accepting the concept of the indivisibility of Truth and the essential unity of existence, a view Gandhi espouses when he says: 'I believe in *advaita*, I believe in the essential unity of man and for that matter of all that lives.'[9] He did not conceive it possible to realize Truth, or accept the concept of the absolute oneness of God, without at the same time recognizing the essential unity of existence. As he says: 'What though we have many bodies? We have but one soul. The rays of the sun are many through refraction. But they have the same source. I cannot, therefore, detach myself from the wickedest soul nor may I be denied identity with the most virtuous.'[10] All men are brothers, therefore, because they share the same *Ātman* and partake of the same reality, the same Truth source.

Gandhi's stress on the importance of self-realization, and seeking to know the true nature of the *Ātman*, and God or Truth, prompts us to look at his indebtedness to the religious tradition in which he was nurtured. In the view of Morarji Desai his concept of Truth is linked to the Hindu concepts of *dharma*, duty, and *ṛta*, the moral law. So his understanding of Truth is ultimately determined by his understanding of the Hindu tradition. This is not to say that insights from other religious traditions do not also inform his apprehension of Truth: his acknowledgment of those influences is explicit enough to substantiate that claim. But it is clear that it is not possible for us to understand what he means by Truth without prior knowledge of the religious tradition in which he was nurtured, and which determined his way of life.

In the Indian religious tradition the concept of God is not the primary concept, and it is interesting to note that it is conspicuously absent from some important streams of Hindu thought. This might account for Gandhi's dissatisfaction with the statement 'God is Truth', which he was content to accept in the first instance, but later came to realize did not accurately reflect his position. His preference for the statement 'Truth is God' not only reflects his position more accurately, but also indicates that he regards the term God to be an appellation for Truth, rather than the term Truth to be a description of God. When he says 'Truth is God', the statement is not inconsistent with his claim that Truth is Being itself. It is consistent also with his rejection of the suggestion that Buddhism is atheistic since, in his view, God is simply the *dharma* of the Buddhists. It also sheds light on the fact that the primary connotation of the term God for him is impersonal rather than personal, and explains why he is able to describe God as the essence of life; pure undefiled consciousness; the unseen power that pervades all things; and as that which is indefinable and formless. If we were to use classical Hindu terminology in this context we might say that when he describes Truth as Being itself, he is propounding the notion of the oneness of *Satya* and *Sat*. These terms are for him two forms of the same concept, though *Satya* clearly preserves the ethical connotation of such terms as *dharma* and *ṛta*.

Gandhi's expressed preference for the impersonal concept of God does not prevent him, however, from recognizing that God is personal for those who need to feel his presence. While he may not consider it necessary, so far as he himself is concerned, for Truth to assume shape or form at any time, he is aware as we have seen, that for some it has to be given a personal connotation in order to meet their specific needs, and when it does so it is called *Īśvara*. This enables him to maintain that it makes little difference whether a devotee conceives of God in personal or impersonal terms, since the one position is not inferior in any way to the other. His readiness to acknowledge that God is all things to all men, enables him to accept both the *Dvaita*, dualistic, and *Viśiṣṭādvaita*, modified non-dualistic, philosophical positions, while at the same time maintaining his own preference for *Advaita*, non-dualism. Two issues are raised here both of which are worthy of comment. The first concerns Gandhi's claim to be an Advaitin and the other his acceptance of the Jain doctrine of *Anekāntavāda*, or what is sometimes referred to as the doctrine of the manyness, or the many-aspectness, of reality. What is significant in this context, however, is the first of these issues, though it has to be acknowledged that the second issue is not unrelated to it. His claim to being an Advaitin clearly does not prevent him from recognizing the possibility of *Dvaita* and *Viśiṣṭādvaita* interpretations of the nature of ultimate reality. But as a self-professed Advaitin he is explicit in his belief in the essential unity of existence, and that when one man gains spiritually, the whole world gains with him, and when he falls, the whole world falls with him to the same extent.[11] His acceptance of the concept of the oneness of humanity, as we have shown, is linked to his belief in the unitary nature of the soul, or Ātman. Man has to become aware of this oneness, and the emphasis with Gandhi is on the need for an educational system that would nurture this form of self-realization, and the relation that exists between the Self, God and Truth.

It is tempting at this point to enquire whether Gandhi lays greater stress on the method of *karma*, action, rather than *jñāna*, knowledge, which is the main characteristic of classical *Advaita*, in seeking self-realization. Our analysis of his concept of true education in relation to *sarvodaya*, however, will show that he advocates the harmonization of the methods of knowledge and action. Knowing the true nature of the Self, the *Ātman*, is coupled in his mind with social action involving *sarvodaya*, a point we shall develop later. So in respect of his desire to know the true nature of the Self, he is in agreement with the tenets of the classical *Advaita* system of Sankara.

Sankara's *Vivekachūdāmani* and his commentary on the *Vedānta Sūtras* provide us with a comprehensive account of his view of *Advaita*, the essence of which is that the inner Self, *Ātman*, is identical with the substratum of the universe, *Brahman*. 'Because there is nothing else whatever but Brahman, and That is the only self-existent Reality, our very Self, therefore art thou that serene, pure, Supreme Brahman, the One without a second.'[12] When we fail to discriminate between the Self and the non-Self, and through ignorance falsely identify ourselves with the physical body, we are bound to the realm of *samsāra*. We need to recognize the oneness of the Self and *Brahman*, and see the Self as indivisible, infinite, and free from all limiting adjuncts such as body, mind and ego.[13] Perfect discrimination, however, is brought about by immediate, intuitive apprehension alone, and achieved in the *samādhi* state wherein all relative ideas are transcended.[14]

If *Brahman-Ātman* is the only self-existent reality, however, it follows that apart from *Brahman* the world has no existence. To maintain otherwise is to acknowledge a reality other than *Brahman*, and from the Advaitic standpoint the world is simply the phenomenal appearance of *Brahman*. This is Sankara's *vivartavāda* doctrine. The rudiments of phenomenal existence belong to *Brahman*, and are variously described as the *māyā* (appearance), *śakti* (power), or the *prakṛti* (nature) of *Brahman*. The world is simply the *lilā* (sport) of *Brahman*, which is a natural activity analogous to breathing and has no other purpose than to fulfil the nature of *Brahman*.[15] As the sun or moon reflected in water becomes manifold, so the one Self or *Brahman*, abiding in all individual beings, appears one and many at the same time.[16] This is not to say that the world is unreal or illusory. It is not unreal because it is the common collective experience of individuals; yet it is not ultimately real because ultimate reality is *Brahman*, the one without a second. To mistake the empirical for the ultimately real is the consequence of *avidyā* (ignorance), which binds man to the world of *saṁsāra*. Sankara's acceptance of the concept of two levels of truth enables him to determine whether something is true or false by taking into consideration the sphere of reality concerned. It would be true to say that the empirical is real when compared with dreams or hallucinations, but it would not be true to say that the empirical is real when what we have in mind is ultimate reality. On the lower level of truth it would be appropriate to refer to *Brahman* as *Īśvara*, and to the world as the creation of *Īśvara*; but on the higher level of truth *Brahman* alone is real, and *Īśvara* and the world are merely apparent. To confuse these two levels of truth would be to engage in what is called *adhyasā*, or illegitimate transference. So, according to Sankara, it would be appropriate to refer to the world as real on the lower level of truth, but since man's final goal is to experience ultimate reality, and the identity of *Atman* and *Brahman*, it is necessary to see the world as it is from the higher level of truth.

A close comparison between Sankara's view and that of Meister Eckhart has been admirably demonstrated by Rudolf Otto who shows that for Eckhart, that which is, is Being itself, which is logically prior to the notion of a Supreme Being or God. Pure Being is indefinable; it is neither this nor that; it is the pure Godhead beyond predication. As one needs to go beyond God into the silent void (*Wüste*) of the Godhead, according to Eckhart,[17] so it is necessary, according to Sankara, to ascend from the lower level of *Īśvara* to the higher level of *nirguṇa Brahman*. The way of liberation for both these thinkers is the way of knowledge, *jñāna*, which is not to be confused with intellectual apprehension or discursive reasoning. It is rather intuitive knowledge, or the insight of the Self within the Self. Sankara speaks of knowing the Self in the Self through the Self, (*ātmani, ātmānam, ātmanā*). That is to say, we realize the identity of *Ātman-Brahman* in the depth of the *ātman*. It is the way in which Sankara and Eckhart emphasize the importance of intuitive knowledge as the means of liberation that, according to Otto, colours their metaphysical concepts with mysticism.[18]

From this brief and albeit inadequate account of the classical *Advaita* system of Sankara, we can see that Gandhi is justified in describing himself as a believer in *Advaita*. He is an Advaitin to the extent that he believes in the essential oneness of all that exists, and his insistence on the oneness of *Satya* and *Sat* indicates that what he has in mind when he uses the term Truth is the traditional Vedāntic concept of *Brahman*. He clarifies this point when he states:

This Truth is not merely the truth we are expected to speak. It is That which alone is, which constitutes the stuff of which all things are made, which subsists by virtue of its own power, which is not supported by anything else but supports everything that exists. Truth alone is eternal, everything else if momentary. It need not assume shape or form, it is pure intelligence as well as pure bliss.[19]

So Truth, for Gandhi, is *sat-cit-ānanda*, or being, consciousness, bliss, which as we have shown, is a description ascribed to *Brahman* in the *Advaita* tradition. So far as his understanding of ultimate reality is concerned, therefore, he is an Advaitin in the classical tradition. But as we have seen, he links the concept of the absolute oneness of Truth to the concept of the unity of humanity. He also claims that whoever recognizes the *Ātman* inhabiting the body to be part of the Supreme *Ātman*, will be prepared to dedicate everything to him.[20] That is, he equates the Self with Truth or God, and insists that prayer is the worship of the Self, the invoking of the divinity within, the petitioning of the 'Higher self, the real self, with which I have not yet achieved complete identification'.[21] For Gandhi, therefore, as for Sankara, to know the Self is to know the Truth, and the true Self is at one with *Brahman*, the substratum of the universe. So when a person is released from the bonds of *avidyā*, or ignorance, through the process of true education, he is, in Gandhi's view, at one with Truth. Sankara insists that the reality underlying the phenomenal world is in no way different from the Self, and Gandhi may be expressing the same idea when he maintains: 'If I exist God exists' and 'If He is not we are nowhere.'[22]

Further comparisons between classical *Advaita* and Gandhi's thought relates to the method whereby an understanding of the oneness of *Atman* and *Brahman* is arrived at. Sankara stresses *jñāna*, knowledge, as the way of liberation from the bonds of nescience and the realm of transitoriness. This is intuitive knowledge rather than what is acquired through the process of ratiocination. If this gives Sankara's metaphysics a mystical flavour, it may be pertinent to ask whether the same mystical approach does not characterize Gandhi's apprehension of Truth. He speaks of knowing the Truth by listening to the inner voice, and when asked on one occasion what he considered Truth to be he replied: 'What the voice within tells you.'[23] This view is firmly rooted in the Indian tradition, and Manu, for example, refers to intuition as one of the four or five authorities on *dharma*. If Gandhi's inner voice can be equated with intuition, then it could be said that he knows the Truth in the Self, through the Self, intuitively, which is the *ātmani, ātmānam, ātmanā* approach of Sankara, and which corresponds to what Eckhart refers to as hearing inwardly the affirmation of Truth as if one is struck by lightning. This is what Otto calls the 'mysticism of introspection', which stresses the need to look within in order to arrive at an intuitive apprehension of Truth.[24] The problem is that different people claim to hear different voices within, which results in different and sometimes contradictory concepts of truth being propounded. Gandhi recognizes that since the human mind works through different media, and that its evolution is not the same for all, it follows that what may be Truth for one person will not necessarily be Truth for another. His own intuitive apprehension of Truth is grounded in the tradition in which he was nurtured, and which determined his way of life. Another apprehension of Truth might be grounded in a different tradition, however, and determined by a different way of life. Hence Gandhi's contention that it would not be appropriate for anyone to claim to hear the inner voice without showing in the first place a measure of self-discipline, single-minded devotion, and indifference to worldly interests. It is because of a lack of self-discipline that untruth abounds in the world; hence his claim: 'All that I can in true humility present to you is that Truth is not to be found by anybody who has not got an abundant sense of humility. If you would swim on the bosom of the ocean of Truth you must reduce yourself to a zero.'[25] This could be interpreted as a recognition of the need to remove by means of true education, all the hindrances inherent in the empirical self, in order that Truth, which is at one with the real Self, might be realized. If so then the same kind of mystical quality found in Sankara is present in Gandhi's apprehension of Truth. He does in fact speak of seeking the Truth within: 'Truth resides in every human heart, and one has to search for it there, and to be guided by truth as one sees it. But no one has the right to coerce others to act according to his own view of truth.'[26]

The possible similarity between Sankara and Gandhi in their apprehension of Truth does not in itself, as Gandhi acknowledges, resolve the problem of different truth claims. The fact is that the ideals which determine the way a man thinks and acts are those which derive from his own way of life. Even if he reduces himself to a zero, his apprehension of truth will still be determined by his awareness of the need to think and act in accordance with certain religious and ethical criteria acquired within his own form of life. So it has to be recognized that what is truth for one person would not necessarily be truth for another. Gandhi acknowledges this fact when he states that perfect Truth is beyond man's grasp. 'We cannot through the instrumentality of this ephemeral body see face to face Truth which is eternal. That is why in the last resort one must depend on faith.'[27] His reference to faith here may explain how it is that he is able to conceive of absolute Truth. In the final analysis it is the result of a mystical apprehension. He speaks of an indefinable mysterious Power pervading everything, which though he does not see, he senses. He calls it a changeless living power that underlies all change and holds all together; it is the 'Spirit of God ... [and] He alone is.'[28]

One might assume that there is a mysticism of introspection, to use Otto's term, in both Sankara and Gandhi, where the stress is on the need to turn within in order to attain a true understanding of the nature of the Self and its relation to Truth or *Brahman*: it is equally true, so far as Gandhi is concerned, to recognize a mysticism of unifying vision. This further phrase of Otto is taken to mean that, in contemplating the multiplicity of the world, one sees the whole in each particular. The distinction between the two types of mysticism, however, is one of analysis only, since in actual fact they interpenetrate one another forming the warp and woof of the fabric of mystical experience.[29] That is, the mystical vision of unity that sees the manifold world as one, can be said to be inextricably bound up with the intuitive apprehension of the nature of Truth. It is certainly possible to show that Gandhi's teaching concerning the unity of existence is related to his concept of the oneness of God or Truth. There may be manifold bodies but there is only one soul, and the One which is the ground of the many is the mysterious power that pervades everything and underlies all change.[30] The manifold things of the world are seen, not in their multiplicity, but in their unity and as changing modes of the One. It is this fact that leads to the claim that Gandhi is an

Advaitin to the extent that he believes in the essential oneness of all that exists.[31] The same point could be expressed differently, namely, that both Gandhi and Sankara conceive of the relation between the many and the one as a relation of dependence, even though their views may differ as to the nature of the reality of the manifold.[32]

Comparisons can clearly be drawn between Gandhi's views and classical *Advaita*, as we have shown, but there are differences between his views and those of Sankara. The latter, for example, insists on knowledge as the sole means of liberation and refers to moral and religious activities as aids to the attainment of *jñāna*.[33] They are regarded as necessary but not sufficient conditions for the realization of the identity of the *Ātman* and the attainment of *mokṣa*. The experience of liberation, of course, could result in a life of social activity and the promotion of love, but it would be because the *jivan mukta*, or the liberated soul, sees all beings in himself and himself in all beings. He promotes love and does good to others because he knows that he is at one with them: his morality rests on metaphysical foundations. Gandhi, on the other hand, stresses *karma* as well as *jñāna* as a way of liberation. For example, he speaks of *ahimsa* and *satya* thus: 'They are like two sides of the same coin, or rather a smooth unstamped metallic disc. Who can say which is the obverse, and which the reverse?'[34]

He regards the practice of *ahimsā* as the means of realizing the goal of Truth. But since means and ends are convertible terms in his philosophy, he can say not only that *ahimsā* leads to the realization of Truth but that to realize Truth is to practise *ahimsā*. It is a two-fold movement as Gandhi explains: 'Ahimsa is my God and Truth is my God. When I look for Ahimsa, Truth says, "Find it through me", When I look for Truth, Ahimsa says "Find it through me".'[35]

In the same way Gandhi refers to the service of humanity as equivalent to the service of God. In order to see the Truth one must be able to love the meanest creature as oneself.[36] His emphasis on *sarvodaya* bears witness to the fact that he recognizes the theonomous nature of humanitarian activity. Through the service of humanity, and the uplift of all, we are brought to a better understanding of Truth; to help the ·helpless, to feed the hungry is to see God. This view will be developed further in our treatment of *sarvodaya* in the following chapter.

Our unity with our fellow-men, in Gandhi's view, presents us with an inescapable moral obligation towards them. We have no right to possess anything while millions remain unclothed and unfed. We should adjust our wants, and undergo voluntary privations if necessary, in order that they may be cared for.[37] So religion is not an individualistic affair; it is not something that concerns man in isolation from his fellow-man; it is not simply a matter of the individual soul seeking liberation and release from the endless cycle of *saṁsāra*. Rather it is bound up with all the activities of life whether they be social, political or economic. 'I am endeavouring to see God through the service of humanity, for I know that God is neither in heaven nor down below, but in everyone.'[38] Here Gandhi is reinterpreting the traditional doctrine of *mokṣa*. He is advocating renunciation *in* action, *karma yoga*, rather than renunciation *of* action. In this respect he is faithful to the teaching of the *Gītā* on the need for detached or selfless action, and goes well beyond the kind of emphasis on activity that one finds in the teaching of Sankara.

While it has to be acknowledged that Gandhi's stress on social and moral activity is not present to the same extent in classical *Advaita*, it could be maintained that his emphasis on *karma* is matched by a similar emphasis on *jñāna*. The practice of *ahiṁsā* and *sarvodaya* rests on metaphysical presuppositions concerning the indivisibility of Truth, the identity of the soul and God, and the essential unity of all that exists. He claims that religion is to morality what water is to seeds in the soil and that a moral life without religion is like a house built on sand.[39] *Karma yoga* may lead to the realization of Truth, but it presupposes at the same time that there is a Truth to be realized. What we might say is that the principles of identity and participation are so closely intertwined that it is difficult sometimes to distinguish between them. His sense of identity with his fellow-men is the primary reason for his participation in social and political affairs. On the other hand, through participation in the service of others he comes to realize his true self and his identity with all that lives. Identity and participation are two sides of the same coin; it is difficult to say which is the obverse and which the reverse. In Hindu terminology we might say that while *jñāna* leads to *karma* it is equally true that *karma* leads to *jñāna*. As a true *karma yogin* Gandhi insists that detached, selfless action, is action in the service of humanity and that *sarvodaya* springs from, and leads to, the realization of the truth of the *Atman-Brahman* identity.[40]

To a great extent Gandhi can be regarded as an Advaitin in the classical mould, and to have derived his views about the nature of the Self, *Ātman*, and its relation to Truth, from the religious tradition in which he was nurtured. It is possible, as we have shown, to point to similarities and differences between his position and that of Sankara. In many ways, however, his thought bears a closer resemblance to the neo-Vedantic teaching of Vivekananda, and we shall have occasion to refer to the similarities between them later. Suffice it at this point to say that his indebtedness to his Hindu religious tradition was significant, and that any understanding of his philosophical position in general, and his educational theories in particular, requires an appreciation of that tradition.

It is as a self-professed Advaitin then, that he equates knowing the Self, the Ātman, with knowing the true nature of Reality, Sat, and with knowing God, or Truth, Satya. For him self-realization is God-realization, which in turn is the realization of Truth. The whole purpose of life, for Gandhi, as we have indicated, is to know the Self, the Ātman, which is akin to knowing the Truth, and realizing God. This is also the goal of true education, 'which helps us to know the atman, our true self, God, and Truth'.[41] When he refers to true education he is speaking of the need for a system of education that would enable us to understand the meaning of the quest for Truth,[42] and at the same time seek to develop the whole man, body, mind and spirit. 'I have always been of the opinion that for true education, strength of the body, mind and heart should be equally and simultaneously developed.'[43] He considers this to be the ultimate goal of education, and insists that it would be a mistake to seek to cultivate the mind in isolation from the body and the spirit. True education is that which cultivates the soul or the spirit, and leads ultimately to the full and complete development of man's body, mind and spirit. He recognizes that it is quite possible for many different types of educational systems to develop the mind and body without much difficulty, but it does not follow that the same was true when it came to the cultivation of the soul, and the development of the spirit. The fact that we may be able to fill a person's mind with a lot of information, no matter how valuable, does not mean that he is thereby educated. A literate mind, he claims, can be like a wild horse pulling us hither and thither, and in order for the intellect to develop effectively it is necessary for the spirit to be properly cultivated. Literacy then is not the primary goal of true education: it is the cultivation of character, and the development of the spirit; it is the education of the heart not the head.[44]

This attitude may go some way towards explaining the reason why Gandhi regards music as essential to true education, and a necessary component of any school curriculum. It has an important part to play in the cultivation of man's spirit because, as it is claimed, it is the language of the soul. In Gandhi's view it involves the concepts of rhythm and order, and has a soothing effect on the minds and hearts of students. It pacifies anger and is helpful 'in leading a man to the vision of God'. Its divine nature is such that when life is permeated with music man is united with God.[45] It is with regret that he notes the neglect of the study of music in India, since, in his view, it occupied such an important place in the educational programme that no curriculum could be considered complete without it. A similar feeling of regret might fill the hearts of those of us who share his ideals, and who are aware of the uplifting character of music, when we contemplate the undue haste with which Universities in the United Kingdom closed down music departments in the 1980s in response to philistine, utilitarian legislation. Gandhi refers to the pacifying and tranquillizing effect of music in his own life: 'I can remember occasions when music instantly tranquillized my mind when I was greatly agitated over something. Music has helped me to overcome anger.'[46] This experience is shared by contemporary educationists, who note the calming and beneficial influence the playing of Mozart symphonies have on students in classroom situations. It is Gandhi's considered view that it would not be appropriate for educationists today to concentrate on the development of the mind or intellect of a person, to the exclusion of his physical and spiritual faculties, since together they constitute an indivisible whole. It would be a mistake also, he believes, to regard literacy as the be-all and end-all of education, or even as the best way to begin to educate a child. Literary training on its own does not contribute to the development of character or add to one's moral stature.[47] It is this attitude to literacy, his insistence on the importance of developing character, his determination to draw out the latent talents of students, and his desire to reveal the qualities of the spirit, that constitute some of the essential aspects of Gandhi's philosophy of education.[48] But the foundation of his educational programme and the basis of his analysis of true education, is his understanding of the nature of Truth. The following chapters will seek to examine the different aspects of his educational philosophy, and at the same time endeavour to draw comparisons with the views of other Hindu reformers, and with the theories of education put forward by prominent exponents of the subject in the western world.

Notes

1. *The Philosophy of Gandhi*, Curzon Press, London and Dublin, 1982
2. *The Selected Works of Mahatma Gandhi*, edited by Shriman Narayan, Navajivan Trust, Ahmedabad, 1968, Vol. VI, pp. 96–7
3. M.K. Gandhi, *Truth is God*, Navajivan Trust, Ahmedabad, 1955, pp. 11, 20
4. Paul Tillich, *Ultimate Concern: Tillich in Dialogue*, Harper and Row, New York, 1965
5. *Selected Works*, Vol. VI, p. 97
6. *Truth is God*, p. 10
7. *Selected Works*, Vol. V, pp 350–3; Vol. VI, pp. 109, 114
8. 'Intimations of Immortality from Recollections of Early Childhood', in William Wordsworth, *Poetical Works*, edited by Thomas Hutchinson, Oxford University Press, Oxford, 1973
9. N.K. Bose, *Selections from Gandhi*, Navajivan Trust, Ahmedabad, 1948, p. 92
10. Ibid.
11. Ibid.
12. *Vivekachudamani of Sri Sankaracharya*, edited by Swami Madhavananda, Advaita Ashrama, Calcutta 1970, p. 98
13. Ibid., pp. 74–6, 145–6
14. Ibid., pp. 131–2
15. *The Vedanta Sutras of Badarayana with the Commentary by Sankara*, translated by George Thibaut, Dover, New York, 1962, Vol. II, pp. 1, 33
16. Ibid., Vol. III, pp. 2, 18
17. Rudolf Otto, *Mysticism East and West*, Macmillan, New York, 1972, pp. 19–23
18. Ibid., p. 34
19. M.K. Gandhi, *In Search of the Supreme*, I, Navajivan Trust, Ahmedabad, 1931, p. 196
20. *Selected Works*, Vol. VI, p. 108
21. *Truth is God*, Navajivan Trust, Ahmedabad, 1955, p. 44
22. Ibid., p. 12
23. Ibid., p. 15
24. *Mysticism East and West*, pp. 50–3
25. *Truth is God*, p. 16
26. *All Men are Brothers*, UNESCO, Paris, 1969, p. 71
27. Ibid., p. 75
28. Ibid., p. 57
29. Ibid., pp. 58–61, 77, 88
30. *Truth is God*, pp. 5–7

31. Margaret Chatterjee, *Gandhi's Religious Thought*, Macmillan, London, 1983, p. 105
32. Gandhi would find it difficult to accept Otto's analysis of the manifold world as the antithesis of the One, the real above the many (*op. cit.*, pp. 63–71). *Avidya* or ignorance may obscure the real nature of the empirical world, but it does not follow that in its manifold nature it is the antithesis of the One. Otto's terminology may be too Hegelian for Gandhi's liking.
33. M. Hiryanna, *Outlines of Indian Philosophy*, George Allen and Unwin, Bombay, 1973, p. 310; *The Vedanta Sutras*, IV, i, p. 15
34. *All Men are Brothers*, p. 81
35. *Truth is God*, p. 4
36. *All Men are Brothers*, p. 58
37. *Truth is God*, p. 28
38. Louis Fischer, editor, *The Essential Gandhi*, Vintage Books, New York, 1962, p. 229
39. *Truth is God*, p. 10
40. S. K. Saxena, 'The Fabric of Self-suffering in Gandhi', *Religious Studies*, XII, 2 (1976), pp. 239–47
41. *The Collected Works of Mahatma Gandhi* (hereafter CWMG), Second Revised Edition, Ministry of Information and Broadcasting, Government of India, New Delhi, 1969–, Vol. 50, p. 182
42. Ibid., p. 185
43. CWMG, Vol. 73, p. 235
44. Ibid., Vol. 47, p. 422; Vol. 26, p. 117; Vol. 56, pp.70, 295
45. Ibid., Vol. 37, pp. 2–3
46. *Selected Works*, Vol. VI, p. 294
47. *All Men are Brothers*, p. 157
48. CWMG, Vol. 30, pp. 58–9 quoted in Raghavan Iyer, *The Moral and Political Writings of Mahatma Gandhi*, Clarendon Press, Oxford, 1987, Vol. 3, pp. 377–9

chapter two

Education and *Sarvodaya*

Gandhi's understanding of Truth, together with his belief in the essential unity of life, have profound social, economic and political implications, and affect his view of the relationship that should exist between man and his fellow-man. This is well illustrated by his teaching on *sarvodaya*, the uplift of all. His concern for the welfare of all is revealed most clearly in his treatment of the untouchables, or Harijans (children of God) as he calls them. In his view they partake of the nature of God, derive from the same Truth source, and have to be regarded as equal with all other members of Hindu society. His depth of feeling on the question of untouchability is such that, if it were to be regarded as an essential part of the Hindu way of life, then he would rather that Hinduism died than that untouchability should live. A religion that showed no concern for the welfare of mankind as a whole did not deserve to be called a religion, in his view, and should Hindus insist on clinging to the concept of untouchability, then he believed that Hinduism might be annihilated.[1] One of the main tenets of Hinduism is belief in the unity of life, and it is not possible to uphold this belief without accepting that all men are brothers. Hence Gandhi's concern with the immorality, injustice, and inhumanity of the practice of untouchability. It is implicit and explicit in everything he says and does, and he is justified to claim that the passion of his life was to be of service to the Harijans of India. By taking up the cause of the untouchables he was challenging the traditional orthodox teaching on caste, and defying centuries of Brahmanic teaching. It is true that initially he approved of a society which recognized functional distinctions based on the different abilities of various members of society. At the outset he saw *varṇāśramadharma*, distinctions related to abilities and duties, as a means of preserving the stability of social life in India. Later, however, he rejected this view on the grounds that it could only lead to the preservation of caste divisions, and thereafter consistently maintained that should untouchability be considered an integral part of the Hindu way of life, he would have to stop calling himself a Hindu. Untouchability, he claimed, was like arsenic in milk, a poison destroying the life of Hindu society. His strength of feeling on the issue led him to seek fundamental changes in the attitude of his fellow-countrymen towards the outcastes of Indian society.

It is interesting to note that a similar attitude to *varṇāśramadharma* is discernible in Radhakrishnan's philosophy. His spiritual interpretation of the universe, and his belief in the oneness of existence, meant that, in his view, all men were bound together in one spirit, and that the common aim of religion in all its forms was to preserve the spiritual values that unite mankind. It follows that for him a life of service and sacrifice was the prerequisite of those who would promote the religion of the spirit. Man's bounden duty was to create and defend those institutions which preserved the ideals of freedom, justice, and truth, and promoted the development of a truly human life. Equally it was man's responsibility to condemn those institutions that would degrade and humiliate the more unfortunate and socially deprived members of society. Clearly the caste system prevalent at the time in Indian society would merit condemnation on that account. But it is significant that while Radhakrishnan explicitly acknowledges the caste system had resulted in much evil and suffering, and had degenerated into an instrument of oppression and intolerance perpetuating inequality, he also maintains that these unfortunate effects were not the main motives for the system. He claims that it was based on sound principles; that it affirmed the infinite diversity of human groups; and that it helped the community 'to live at peace with itself and in harmony with others'.[2] When he makes this point he has in mind the system of trade guilds whereby one's sphere of work is clearly delineated, and in this respect he shares the views initially held by Gandhi concerning *varṇāśramadharma*, namely, that there are certain functions and duties which are related to one's status in society. In Radhakrishnan's view, no notion of inferiority or superiority is implied by these divisions: they were to be regarded simply as a matter of custom, no matter how crude they might appear to us. It could be argued, however, that while functional distinctions, based on the differing abilities of different members of society, contributed significantly towards the stability of social life in India, it was only a short step from acceptance of functional distinctions to toleration of those caste divisions that led eventually to the development of the concept of untouchability. This is explicitly acknowledged by Gandhi, and is implicit in what Radhakrishnan has to say about stereotyping people without regard to their special aptitudes and natural endowment, a practice which, in his view, could lead ultimately to a life of enslavement for some.[3]

Gandhi's fight on behalf of the untouchables was matched by his enlightened attitude towards women. In the traditional Hindu system a woman's lot was not an enviable one, and nothing was more shocking, in Gandhi's view, than man's abuse of the female sex. But his argument is that provided they remained true to their nature they were capable of wielding great power. They were without doubt the nobler sex, the personification of self-sacrifice, and the incarnation of *ahiṁsā*. They had greater endurance than men, and an infinite capacity for love. They were capable also of doing much for the cause of Truth and for the art of peace in the world.[4] So *sarvodaya* had as much to do with the status of women as with the treatment of the untouchables in Hindu society, and was concerned with establishing the basic human rights of both groups. One of the primary ways in which those rights could be restored, so far as Gandhi was concerned, was by the provision of equality of opportunity in the field of education. It is my contention that his philosophy of education is directly related to, if not determined by, his belief in *sarvodaya*, which in turn is rooted in his belief in the essential unity of mankind, and the indivisibility of Truth.

The concept of *sarvodaya*, as we have seen, points to the universal uplift of mankind, and not just the greatest happiness of the greatest number as the utilitarians would advocate. The latter would gladly sacrifice the happiness of forty-nine per cent of the population if the good of fifty-one per cent could be promoted. Not so *sarvodaya*, which might well be regarded as a more dignified and humane philosophy than utilitarianism. The believer in *ahiṁsā* would 'strive for the good of all and die in the attempt to realise the ideal...be willing to die, so that the others may live. The utilitarian to be logical will never sacrifice himself. The absolutist will even sacrifice himself.'[5] It could be argued, however, that *sarvodaya* is an unattainable ideal and that, in an imperfect world, it would be better to settle for the more limited ideal of utilitarianism. One response to this argument is that the morality and justice of a philosophy do not depend upon its attainability, and that actions aimed at the uplift of all are regarded as right for reasons other than consequential. By insisting that the moral value and justification of an action is to be found in its consequences, the utilitarian is at odds with those proponents of *sarvodaya* who regard the creation of equity and justice in human life as important goals in themselves. Furthermore, utilitarians, as committed empiricists, might be well advised to recognize the fact that what makes some people happy is that they are committed to a cause, and that their happiness derives from something other than the pursuit of happiness.[6]

This criticism of the utilitarian approach supports Gandhi's contention that *sarvodaya* displays greater dignity and humanity than utilitarianism. It is interesting to note also that when he translated Ruskin's book *Unto This Last* into Gujarati, Gandhi used the term *sarvodaya* as the title. The book influenced him greatly because it embodied much of what *sarvodaya* meant to him as his summary of its contents indicates: the good of the individual is contained in the good of all; all men have the same right to earn a living from their labour; and a life of labour where one works with one's hands is a life worth living.

It was his awareness of the oneness of humanity, and his kinship with all men, that governed Gandhi's concern for the welfare of all, and determined his attitude to the Harijans and women in Indian society. By the very use of the term Harijans he is suggesting that the untouchables derive from *Brahman* in the same way as the Brahmins, Kṣatriyas and Vaiśyas, and the Śūdras. If that is the case, then Harijans were in no way different from other members of Indian society, and should not be regarded as outcastes. They partook of the nature of God in the same way as other Hindus, and for that reason should be considered at one with mankind as a whole. The same principle applied to women whose status in the traditional Hindu system, as we have suggested, was not an enviable one. They had been reduced to the status of second-class citizens by laws formulated and introduced by men, and as a consequence they were made to feel inferior in every respect. They had been dominated by men to such an extent that they had come to be regarded as mere objects, which had led to the substitution of what Martin Buber would call an I-It relationship for an I-Thou relationship,[7] and had established a custom that decreed that even the most inferior man, despite his worthlessness, could enjoy an undeserved measure of superiority over them. As Gandhi claims: 'Of all the evils for which man has made himself responsible, none is so degrading, so shocking or so brutal as his abuse of the better half of humanity—to me, the female sex ....'[8] His contention is that wives, for example, should not be treated like 'dolls' or 'objects of indulgence', but rather as honoured comrades on life's journey. They deserved to be treated with respect by their husbands, and be allowed to acquire a liberal education,[9] Their illiteracy was a direct result of the inferior status with which they had been unjustly branded by tradition.[10] Yet women, in his view, had greater moral power, courage, and endurance than men; a greater capacity for love and suffering; and consequently the ability to do more for the cause of truth and *ahiṁsā*. He makes his point thus: 'If non-violence is the law of our being, the future is with woman...God has vouchsafed to woman the power of non-violence more than to man. It is all the more effective because it is mute.'[11]

Gandhi's attitude to women, like his attitude to the untouchables, springs from his conviction that we are all one and share the same Ātman. The unity of mankind derives from the unity of Truth or God, and since we all partake of the same reality, *Brahman*, it is not possible for one person to be degraded without another suffering. Hence the need for *sarvodaya*, the uplift of all, a task which is effected in a very special way by means of education. It follows that education should be universally available, and include women and untouchables. It should be available to all because it provides a necessary, if not sufficient, conditions for ameliorating the plight, and elevating the status, of the less fortunate members of Hindu society . Education would be in vain if we failed to 'learn the art of feeling one with the poorest in the land.'[12] So for this reason scholarships should be provided in high schools and colleges for the untouchables of both sexes,[13] and wealthy Hindus should play their part in this respect to ensure that monetary help was available to enable them to benefit from higher education.[14] Nothing was likely to succeed better than education in liberating the mind, setting people free from bondage, enriching character, increasing intelligence, and adding to the wealth of the nation.[15]

It is not without significance, as we have noted, that Gandhi should have sub-titled his Autobiography *The Story of My Experiments with Truth*, because it is clear that he sought to live his life in the spirit of Truth and in accordance with the religious and ethical ideals of the Hindu way of life. No distinction can be drawn between Truth (*Satya*) and Reality (*Sat*), in his view, or between Reality and the Self (*Ātman*), and in true Advaitin fashion he recognizes the identity of *Ātman-Brahman*. The Self within is at one with the substratum of the universe, *Brahman*, which in turn is at one with Truth. It follows that belief in the identity of *Ātman-Brahman*, and the indivisibility of Truth, involves belief in the oneness of humanity. We may have many bodies yet we have but one Soul or *Ātman*. These metaphysical presuppositions, as we have endeavoured to show, inform Gandhi's thought, and derive from the Hindu way of life in which he was nurtured. They indicate clearly the interrelation of religion and morality in Hindu thought, and point to the fact that as human beings we have an inescapable moral obligation to our fellow-men. This is well illustrated by Gandhi's emphasis on *sarvodaya*, and his abiding concern for the lowly status of the Harijans and women in Indian society. He is scathing about the shameful treatment of women and argues that their suppression had led to the paralysis, *ardhangavayu*, of society. He advocates that female freedom should be cherished just as much as male freedom, and that the full dignity and status of women should be restored.[16] He saw the need ultimately for the total abolition of the caste system, the practice of child marriage, the dowry system, enforced widowhood, and the custom of purdah, all of which he believed to be harmful to the groups concerned, and to the moral and spiritual growth of the nation.[17] Radical social changes were required to improve the lot of the outcastes and women in Hindu society, and, in his view, only far-reaching action in the field of education could bring about the desired and necessary improvements in the Hindu way of life.

In this respect Gandhi echoes Vivekananda's teaching, who on social matters develops in thought and action the far-reaching implication of those metaphysical beliefs common to them both. They are beliefs rooted in Vedāntic philosophy, and watered by views garnered from other religious traditions. Vivekananda saw clearly that there was need for reform of the orthodox treatment of outcastes, and the traditional Hindu attitude to privilege and wealth. He recognized, as Gandhi did, that religion applied not just to one dimension of a man's life, but to every aspect of his existence. Both rejected the attempt to compartmentalize religion, and at the same time succeeded in removing the demarcation line between the sacred and the secular. Both saw God in the face of the poor and needy: Vivekananda refers to him as *Daridrānāryan*, God of the poor, while Gandhi speaks of finding God in the hearts of the needy, and seeing him as the bread of life for starving men. Vivekananda's enthusiasm for social reform is prompted by the plight of the poor:

The poor and the miserable are for our salvation, so that we may serve the Lord, coming in the shape of the diseases, coming in the shape of the lunatic, the leper, and the sinner! Bold are my words; and let me repeat that it is the greatest privilege in our life that we are allowed to serve the Lord in all these shapes.[18]

Gandhi views the gift of food to a starving man as a gift to God. He argues that he 'may as well place before a dog over there the message of God as before those hungry millions who have no lustre in their eyes and whose only God is their bread'.[19] Vivekananda saw that the crying need of India was not religion but bread, and he considered it an insult to offer starving people religion, or to teach them metaphysics, when what they really needed was to be saved from starvation.[20] He believed poverty to be the root evil of India, and, in his view, one of the main solutions to the problem was the provision of education for the masses.[21]

The social, economic, and political implications of Gandhi's emphasis on *sarvodaya*, as we have suggested, are far-reaching. His economic policy, for example, is people-oriented and rejects those developments that dehumanize and degrade people's lives such as unbridled industrialization. His alternative educational programme in the social sphere fosters rather than undermines the cultural heritage of the nation. His political goal of *swaraj* or self-rule is aimed at promoting self-respect and strengthening the determination of the Indian people to accept responsibility for managing their own affairs. He refuses to draw a hard-and-fast line between religion and politics on the grounds that religion should govern every form of activity, and that to speak of leaving religion for politics or politics for religion was nonsense. To be truly religious, he claims, means taking an active part in political life. A politics permeated by religion would be a politics dedicated to serving the needs of humanity, and preserving human

rights and individual freedom. We shall have occasion to look further
at the economic and political implications of *sarvodaya* in a later
chapter; our concern here is with its social implications.

It is possible to maintain that the aims of *sarvodaya*, and its social
implications, are not inconsistent with the aims of the liberation
theologians who are concerned with freeing man from the shackles of
injustice, exploitation and oppression. Gustavo Gutierrez speaks of
finding God in the temple of humanity, and in our dealings with our
fellow-men, while Juan Luis Segundo emphasizes that the first step in
the process of liberation is commitment to the socially oppressed.
Gandhi starts from his understanding of Truth and insists that religion
cannot be an individualistic affair, or something that concerns man
in isolation from his fellow-man. He sees it rather as bound up with
the whole of life, including social and political activities, and claims
'to see God through the service of humanity'.[22] This is similar to the
sentiment expressed by Gutierrez, that to do justly, to love mercy, to
feed the hungry, and uplift the oppressed, is what loving God means.[23]
Both share a sense of identity with their fellow-men, which is one of
the reasons for their participation in social, political and economic
affairs. On the other hand it is through participation in the service of
others that they come to realize the true nature of God. There is no
doubt that Gandhi's concept of religion involved helping the helpless,
alleviating poverty and starvation, and seeking the uplift of all men,
sarvodaya. His passion to serve the underprivileged is such that he
claims to find God in the hearts of the poor and in a stark and poignant
phrase refers to God as the belly of the starving man.[24] Our unity
with our fellow-men in the bonds of Truth, Gandhi argues, presents
us with an inescapable moral obligation towards them and shows
clearly the inescapable relation that exists between morality and
religion. We have to adjust our wants and needs, and be prepared to
suffer privation if necessary, in order to provide for our brethren who
are unclothed and unfed. What can be said here is that the social
philosophy of Gutierrez and Gandhi is people-oriented; it is concerned
with the well-being and uplift of all people.

Gandhi is close to the liberation theologians in respect of political
activities also, in that he was not averse to effecting the transformation
of social structures through non-violent means. Liberation in the
Indian context meant for him *swaraj*, self-rule, which involved not
only dedication to the well-being of India, but also commitment to

the service of humanity.[25] He regarded the traditions, language, and
the cultural heritage of his country, to be of great significance, and for
that reason he resisted those forces of the British Raj that tended to
undermine its traditions, and deprive his fellow-countrymen of their
cultural roots. In his view, it was a policy that inflicted a moral and
intellectual injury on the Indian nation and was consequently a
violation of Truth. So *swaraj* for him had a theological foundation; it
had its roots in metaphysical beliefs about Truth and God.
Nationalistic aspirations were entirely justified; self-determination was
a basic human right and people ought not to be deprived of the right
to govern themselves. We shall have occasion to examine this concept
at greater length in a later chapter. What is evident from all that has
been said hitherto is that Gandhi is advocating in the social and political
spheres a theology of liberation. His starting point may differ from that
of the liberation theologians, but his goal is similar, namely, the creation
of a just society where injustice gives way to justice, inhumanity to
humanity, and exploitation to freedom.

We have referred to the importance of education in Gandhi's
attempt to achieve his goal of improving the lot of women, and the
status of the Harijans, by giving them a more elevated role than they
had hitherto enjoyed in Hindu society. So when he expressed his views
on education and advocated a system of compulsory primary education
for everyone, he had in the forefront of his mind those unfortunate
members of Hindu society whose basic human rights had been ignored.
He saw clearly that one of the ways in which their rights could be
restored was by providing them with equality of opportunity in the
field of education. This applied particularly to women who had
hitherto been sadly neglected by those responsible for providing
education in India. He was realistic enough, however, to see that no
compulsory system of basic, mass education was likely to succeed unless
it was economically self-sufficient, and included some form of
vocational training. He recognized that economic self-sufficiency
could in part be derived from the sale of crafts produced by the students,
but he advocated vocational training, and the teaching of handicrafts,
not only because of the limited, economic benefits that such an
approach would provide, but also because it provided a more balanced
form of education, and better prepared a person for life. It gave him
the training necessary to enable him to earn his living, for example,
and provide for his family. It was impossible, in Gandhi's view, as we

have seen, to exaggerate the harm done to the youth of India by the notion that somehow it was not fitting for them to labour with their hands in order to earn their living. His advocacy of the spinning-wheel was in this respect essentially symbolic. It underlined his belief in the dignity of labour; symbolized his identification with the poorest of the nation; emphasized the importance of self-reliance as the basis of self-rule; and pointed to the significance of *khadi* and *swadeshi* in the quest for *swarāj*. It is understandable, therefore, that he should regard the craft of hand-spinning as a sacrament, and that he should view the effort made to master the craft as adding significantly to the strength of the nation.[26] His belief in the importance of education in the quest for *swaraj* will be examined in a later chapter.

Notes

1. *The Collected Works of Mahatma Gandhi* (hereafter, CWMG), Second Revised Edition, Ministry of Information and Broadcasting, Government of India, New Delhi, Vol. 56, p. 290
2. Sarvepalli Radhakrishnan, *The Hindu View of Life*, George Allen and Unwin, London, 1964, pp. 93, 97–9
3. Sarvepalli Radhakrishnan, *Indian Religions*, Vision Books, New Delhi, 1979, pp. 85, 87
4. *The Selected Works of Mahatma Gandhi*, Navajivan Trust, Ahmedabad, 1969, VI, p. 486
5. *Selected Works*, Vol. VI, pp. 230–1
6. J.J.C. Smart and Bernard Williams, *Utilitarianism For and Against*, Cambridge, 1973, pp. 78, 137, 148
7. Martin Buber, *I and Thou*, translated by Ronald Gregor Smith, T. & T. Clark, Edinburgh, 1937, 1953
8. *All Men are Brothers*, compiled and edited by Krishna Kripalani, UNESCO, 1958, 1969, p. 161.
9. CWMG, Vol. 75, p. 155
10. Ibid., Vol. 68, p. 341
11. *All Men are Brothers*, pp. 162, 167
12. CWMG, Vol. 56, p. 290
13. Ibid., Vol. 51, p. 402; Vol. 52, p. 68
14. Ibid., Vol. 51, p. 348
15. Ibid., Vol. 46, p. 101
16. Ibid., Vol. 39, p. 416

17. *Selected Works*, VI, pp. 489, 494; *All Men are Brothers*, p. 161
18. *The Complete Works of Swami Vivekananda*, Vol. III, pp. 245–6
19. N. K. Bose, *Selections from Gandhi*, Navajivan Trust, Ahmedabad, 1948, p. 47; *Selected Works*, Vol. V, p. 443
20. *The Complete Works*, Vol. I, p. 20
21. Ibid., Vol. IV, p. 481
22. Louis Fischer, *The Essential Gandhi*, Vintage Books, New York, 1962, p. 229
23. Gustavo Gutierrez, *A Theology of Liberation*, SCM Press, London, 1974, p. 200
24. *Selected Works*, Vol. V, p. 443
25. Ibid., Vol. VI, p. 247
26. Raghavan Iyer, *The Moral and Political Writings of Mahatma Gandhi*, Clarendon Press, Oxford, 1987, Vol 3, p. 382

chapter three

Constructive Programme

The constructive programme of education which Gandhi sought to promote was universal in the sense that it involved both basic and adult education. Basic education had implications for millions of children in India for without it their education would have been impossible.[1] Without adult education, on the other hand, the status of the Harijans and women in Indian society would have remained unchanged.[2] It was Gandhi's belief that adult education had been woefully neglected by the Congress in the past, and in a speech on the significance and meaning of his constructive programme, he pointed out that it was essential for adults to be politically educated in addition to being provided with a literary education. The primary aim of the programme was the elimination of illiteracy in India, and in pursuit of that goal he advocated that women be allowed to receive a liberal education, and be treated as honoured comrades along with men rather than as objects of indulgence.[3] He deplored their shameful treatment in the Indian society of the day, and urged that their dignity and status be restored.[4] To this end he argued that together with their male counterparts they should be allowed to benefit from the constructive programme by being provided with scholarships in high schools and colleges.[5] He also urged that they be given technical training[6] with financial assistance from well-to-do Hindus, who, by so helping them, would be promoting *sarvodaya* in practical terms.[7] It is significant that when asked, during a discussion with representatives of municipalities and local educational boards, whether schemes for adult education should aim at promoting literacy, or imparting useful and practical knowledge, and whether they should include the education of women, he replied that mass illiteracy was in itself a sin and a shame in India and ought to be eradicated. This included in particular female illiteracy, which derived from the inferior status they had been unjustly accorded by tradition.[8] The entire educational system of India, in his view, needed to be radically overhauled, in order that an alternative system could be devised that would cater for the masses. No system was acceptable that did not provide for adult education alongside the education of children, and that did not give pride of place to the use of the vernacular as the medium of instruction.[9] We shall have occasion to examine the importance of the vernacular in his philosophy of education in greater detail in a later chapter. Suffice it to say at this point that, in his view, the system of education prevailing in India at the time did not meet the needs of the people because of the excessive importance attached to the teaching of English, which had 'cast upon the educated classes a burden which has maimed them for life and made them strangers in their own land.'[10] He argued that the hypnotic spell cast by English tutors should be discarded, and that a country like India needed above all a system of education that would be self-sustaining. American students had shown the way by engaging in different kinds of remunerative work in order to pay for their education,[11] and should Indian students follow their example it would help them to become more mindful of their morals.[12]

If we enquire of Gandhi why he introduces the subject of morality in this context, and why he lays such stress on the need for schools to be self-sustaining and self-supporting, he reminds us of the high cost of education in a country like India. In a pointed address to students in Karachi, on 5 February 1929, he poses the question:

... have you ever considered at what cost to the country you are receiving your education? As students of economics you might know that the fees that you pay hardly cover a fraction of the amount that is spent on education out of the public exchequer. Have you ever thought as to where the rest of the money comes from? It comes from the pockets of the poor, the walking skeletons of Orissa. They do not know what college education means, their eyes lack lustre; their bodies are emaciated...Nor should you forget that your education is financed out of the notorious 'excise revenue' which spells the moral ruin of so many of your fellow-countrymen.[13]

Such a view would appeal greatly to those who advocate that higher education should be paid for by those who participate in it and not subsidized by the state. Gandhi's considered view is that by making education self-sustaining students might become less self-concerned and restless, and develop instead a measure of mental poise and moral excellence.[14] It is not immediately clear why students should have been self-concerned and restless in the first place, unless Gandhi had in mind the fact that educational fees paid by the state were not always forthcoming, or else that the students themselves might feel uneasy at being supported by 'the walking skeletons of Orissa'. Whatever the reason, it is his view that greater mental poise and stability would result from a self-sustaining system of education, as would a feeling of moral rectitude when students assumed personal responsibility for the cost of their own education.

A system of education where self-reliance was paramount necessarily involved the introduction of crafts into the school curriculum, so far as Gandhi was concerned, and it is of some significance that he believed the teaching of handicrafts should be given pride of place in the educational programme of children. In this respect it is possible for comparisons to be drawn between Gandhi's constructive programme and the Montessori educational method, as we shall show in a later chapter, and this is nowhere more evident than in his analysis of the requirements of basic education. In his view its primary purpose is to transform the lives of village children and link them to what is permanent and best in Indian society.[15] In propounding this view he was influenced by two considerations. In the first place he had a high regard for the creative skills involved in producing artistic objects, and secondly, he believed that the sale of such objects produced by students might enable a school to become economically self-supporting.[16] In developing his theory of basic education he makes the point that it would not be impossible to communicate the skills of reading and writing, and the rudiments of history, geography and mathematics, alongside the teaching of crafts. He is not convinced, for instance, that it was to a child's advantage to be forced to learn the alphabet, or to read books, at a tender age. Clearly he is attracted to the value of the oral communication of knowledge, and as such he is lending his support to the long-established traditions relating to the literary heritage of India. 'Literary training by itself', he claims, 'adds not an inch to one's moral height and character-building is independent of literary training.'[17]

This view of basic education may have derived from Gandhi's painful memories of his own early education. But his attempt to relate education, in the generally accepted sense of the term, to practical activity, especially in the primary stages, shows that he is convinced of the need to combine the art of acquiring knowledge with the acquisition of practical skills. It would appear that this is the kind of approach some educationists today consider to be necessary for a person to live an effective and satisfying life. They believe that certain interdependent elements are the necessary prerequisites of a basic educational programme, namely, a positive attitude to work on the one hand, and the acquisition of the skills of literacy and numeracy on the other. They recognize, however, that there has long been what they describe as a tyranny of the intellect because of the emphasis that has always been placed on the importance of intellectual skills, but they also acknowledge that the love of working with one's hands is difficult to suppress. It is involvement in skilled activity through the use of his hands that gives a child great joy in the early period of his life, and they argue that it ought not to be too difficult to reinstate the concept of the dignity of this kind of creative activity in modern educational programmes. Such a restructuring of the educational curriculum, it is claimed, might well result in the release of a great amount of creative energy.[18] Gandhi, as we have seen, combines these two prerequisites of a balanced educational programme when he suggests that the acquisition of the basic skills of literacy and numeracy should go hand in hand with the creative activity involved in the production of crafts. The teaching of handicrafts for him was the pivot and centre of the whole educational programme. It cultivated the creative instincts, which was sufficient reason in itself to advocate that training in handicrafts should go hand in hand with the training of the intellect.[19] He goes on to maintain that such training should occupy 'the primary place in a scheme of national education,' for the ultimate aim is the resuscitation of the villages of India.[20] As he explains:

My plan to impart primary education through the medium of village handicrafts like spinning and carding, etc., is thus conceived as the spearhead of a silent social revolution fraught with the most far-reaching consequences. It will provide a healthy and moral basis of relationship between the city and the village and thus go a long way towards eradicating some of the worst evils of the present social insecurity and poisoned relationship between the classes.[21]

The positive attitude to work, and the creative activity enjoined in the constructive programme delineated by Gandhi, is not unrelated to what he has to say about the dignity of labour. If it was sound educational practice to combine the acquisition of intellectual knowledge with the creative activity involved in the production of crafts, it was also sound social practice to combine mental and physical activities. Brahmin intellectuals in the past readily engaged in manual labour; the tendency of contemporary intellectuals to be contemptuous of soiling their hands by engaging in physical labour, was in marked contrast to the earlier practice which upheld the concept of the dignity of labour. So Gandhi was proposing something quite revolutionary when he referred to the sacramental nature of manual labour, by means of which we were identifying ourselves with the lower strata of society, and he was right to point out that it had the potential to revolutionize the structure of society and revitalize village life.[22]

The creative activity enjoined in the constructive programme of education is not unrelated either to the emphasis Gandhi placed on the importance of the spinning-wheel. When he expressed the desire to make the spinning-wheel the foundation on which to build a sound village life, and the centre around which all other activities would revolve,[23] he was indicating that it was a symbol of self-respect, self-help, and self-reliance, as well as a pointer to the dignity of labour, and a symbol of economic self-sufficiency.[24] His advocacy of the wearing of *khadi* and his support for the concept of *swadeshi*, which in this context might be defined as a determination to find the necessities of life in India, and to choose home-produced goods to the exclusion of the foreign-produced variety, can be compared with his desire to make his educational programme self-sufficient. The ultimate aim in both cases was the resuscitation of the villages of India and the enrichment of the lives of the ordinary people. His speech to students at Khadi Vidyalaya college on the occasion of the distribution of certificates, combined his economic and educational ideals. He referred to some of the drawbacks of the modern educational system of India as he saw it, such as its tendency to be rather mechanical in preparing students for examinations which only befitted them for clerkships in the Indian Civil Service. It made no difference to the wealth of the nation whether the students passed their examinations or not, and it was, in any event, a most expensive form of education for the government to maintain. In contrast to this, the purpose of education provided at Khadi Viyalaya college was to stimulate originality and contribute to the wealth of the nation. The revival of the Khadi industry for which the college stood, meant that it sought to cultivate the spirit of service, and to adapt all knowledge acquired to the desired goal of the country's freedom.[25]

Not that Gandhi's advocacy of the spinning-wheel escaped criticism. In an interview to the Stead's Review in 1924 he was asked whether he would elevate the spinning-wheel above the need for the elementary education of the masses. His reply to the criticism implicit in the question was: 'Why should I wait for my country to be educated in the European sense, before saving it from starvation? ... They want bread and butter before education.'[26] It was for the same reason that he rejected the concept of compulsory education funded by the state. Yet at the same time he insisted that even after *swarāj* every effort should be made to promote the value of literacy by means of voluntary education.[27]

A similar stress on the need for education to combine self-development and self-fulfilment with the acquisition of skills, is contained in Stewart Sutherland's Hume Lecture on the price of ignorance.[28] Sutherland asks the question how costly it would be if we did not accept the necessity to pay the price for knowledge. His argument is that the economic consequences of ignorance would be great indeed, but that the denial of the opportunity of self-fulfilment would be even greater. He follows Kant in maintaining that the purpose of education concerns our very identity as human beings—which is reminiscent of what Gandhi says concerning the need to know the true nature of the self—and that man only becomes fully human through education. What this implies is that not only is knowledge valuable in itself, and highly prized for its own sake, but that ignorance is costly in the extreme. The author recognizes that training has its proper place in education; that there is need for teachers, doctors, and dentists to be trained in order that the community might be served. Training then has its proper place, but at the same time it has to be acknowledged that it does not provide the kind of understanding which is 'able to distinguish truth from error, good argument from bad argument; to know when to adapt techniques to new environments, when to revise or discard some long-held assumptions and when opinion is masquerading as knowledge'.[29] The greatest price of ignorance is to ignore or neglect the kind of education which combines self-development and the acquisition of skills, and which leads to the development of a society committed 'to the pursuit of truth and the canons of reasonable judgement and argument'.[30] It is beyond doubt that Gandhi would be in complete agreement with this assessment of the purpose of education.

It would be a mistake to assume, however, he was in any way enthusiastic about propounding his views on education. He had never aspired to academic distinction, and in fact was extremely hesitant about stating his theories for fear of being ridiculed. He did not believe that he was in any way qualified to lecture educational experts on the purpose of education. But his quest for Truth, which is related to his belief in the unity of existence, and which finds practical expression in his concern for the uplift and service of humanity, *sarvodaya*, enabled him to overcome his fears. When he eventually expressed his views on education, and advocated a system that would provide primary education for everyone, he had in the forefront of his mind those unfortunate members of Hindu society whose basic human rights had been ignored. He saw quite clearly that one of the ways in which their rights could be restored was by the provision of equality of opportunity in the field of education. This applied particularly to women who had hitherto been sadly neglected by those responsible for providing education in India. Gandhi was realistic enough, however, to see that no system of basic education was likely to succeed unless it acquired a measure of economic self-sufficiency. This was one of the reasons why he favoured vocational training, because it taught students the value of an occupation, which enabled them to pay for the education provided. The same was true of his support for the measure of economic self-sufficiency that could be derived from the sale of crafts produced by students. Yet he advocated vocational training and the teaching of handicrafts not only because of the economic benefits that such an approach would provide, but also because it was sound educational practice to combine the acquisition of intellectual knowledge with the creative activity involved in the production of crafts. He therefore favoured the correlation of handicrafts and literacy in the field of primary education, because it cultivated the creative instincts, promoted self-reliance and encouraged self-sufficiency. It was impossible, in his view, to exaggerate the harm done to the youth of India by the notion that somehow it was not fitting for them to labour with their hands in order to earn their living, for to despise manual labour was to demoralize the nation.[31] This was the main reason why he viewed the craft of hand-spinning as a sacrament. Nothing was more ennobling because it symbolized one's identification with the poorest of the nation, and by making the effort to learn the craft we were adding to the strength of the nation.[32]

The spinning-wheel was the symbol *par excellence* of self-reliance and *swarāj* for Gandhi, and in a speech at a municipal reception at Berhampur on 29 March 1921, he maintained that the resources for national education under *swarāj* would come from the spinning-wheel. The aim should always be self-reliance, with crafts as much an essential part of education as Hindi.[33] This view was echoed in his speech at a teachers' training camp at Brindaban on 4 May 1939, when he claimed that a man was not intelligent if his intellect was not correlated with his hands.[34] In a discussion session with trainee teachers in the same year he was asked whether it was not inevitable that handicrafts would give way in due course to industrialization, and whether his concept of basic education really met the needs of India. In his reply he claimed that there would always be villages in India, and that the education of the country had to be revolutionized in the way he was suggesting in order that the brain might be educated through the hand. In the past the policy had been to add handicrafts to the existing curriculum, almost as an afterthought, but this was a mistaken idea. It was necessary to correlate crafts and intellectual knowledge, and to recognize that the provision of a form of education that combined crafts and literacy was the right way forward. It was necessary also that students should be taught the essence of morality, and develop the kind of understanding that would enable them to discriminate between good and bad, right and wrong.[35] Religious education had its proper place in this respect, and his views on that subject will be dealt with at greater length in a later chapter.

It is worthy of note that among his followers Vinoba Bhave was foremost in support of his educational programme. He approved of the policy of making education self-supporting through the teaching and sale of handicrafts in schools, for example,[36] and is commended by Gandhi for producing a textbook which regarded spinning as 'the handicraft *par excellence* which lends itself to being effectively used for basic education.'[37] Bhave's contribution to the philosophy of education, and his support of Gandhi's policies, will be examined later. What is interesting to note at this point is that, in Gandhi's view, both primary and higher education were more widespread in India prior to British rule than subsequently. That being the case a boycott of Government-run schools, should it be implemented, did not mean that students would necessarily forfeit educational opportunities. True they might lack 'grand school buildings built with the money soaked in the blood of the poor', but, on the other hand, they would not receive the kind of education that would simply destroy their independence.[38] This devastating comment by Gandhi is an indication of the depth of his feeling on the subject, and his total rejection of the alien form of education imposed on India by the British. We shall have occasion to comment further on this aspect of his philosophy when we examine his views on *swarāj*.

What he has to say about primary education applies equally to his view of higher education. Asked on one occasion whether primary education should be for the villages, secondary education for the cities, and higher education for those who would take up work in the social services, he replied that he saw no reason why villagers should be satisfied with primary education, and that they had as much right as anyone else to receive secondary and higher education. So he approves of the provision of higher education for all who desired it, and who might benefit from it, but he does not agree that it should be paid for by the state, or that it was the responsibility of the state to find the money to establish universities. His view is that university education should be in line with basic education; if people wanted it, they should supply the funds for it. This attitude, as we have seen, would meet with the approval of many today who feel that it is not the responsibility of the state to support financially those who wish to proceed to higher education, and also those who would advocate the provision of loans rather than grants to enable students to study for degrees. Gandhi, however, goes further when he maintains that universities, like schools and colleges, should be self-supporting. That is, he extends to higher education the principle of self-reliance and self-sufficiency that he claims should operate in primary education, and by so doing he is proposing a form of university education which he believes to be consistent with the needs of India. When he suggests that colleges and universities should be attached to industries, which should pay for the training of the graduates they need, he is advocating the principle of what we would call today sandwich courses, and is clearly very contemporary in his approach.[39] What his view implies is that there should be careful monitoring of curricula by university authorities so that their teaching programmes are sufficiently vocationally oriented to produce the type of graduates both industry and society need.[40] Though whether he envisaged that the link between industry and higher education should apply even in conditions of economic recession, which would automatically adversely affect a student's educational programme, is not at all clear. It is clear is that he regarded some areas of education in art subjects, as a 'sheer waste' which, according to him, 'has resulted in unemployment among the educated classes'. The exception to this waste, it would seem was music, given the high place he accords to it for its benefecial effects on students.[41] This is a sentiment in line with that expressed by certain United Kingdom politicians, who viewed the study of art subjects, including history and music, as a luxury. Gandhi's view may well have been a reflection on the non-vocational nature of art subjects in general, and if so it could be said that, in common with those political counterparts in the United Kingdom, he had a limited understanding of the nature and purpose of higher education in the arts. On the other hand, it could be argued that what he was proposing was a system of education that in his view best fitted the needs of his country. Education would perform a disservice to Indian society as a whole if it produced graduates who were contemptuous of manual labour and disinclined to soil their hands, or who considered it beneath their dignity to engage in menial tasks that other less able people could do quite effectively.[42] It is ironic, to say the least, that the British educational system in India succeeded in creating an educated elite who were inclined to despise those of their fellow-countrymen who 'cut wood and carried water', and who were content to be what the system intended them to be, namely, clerks and interpreters in the Indian Civil Service.[43]

Whitehead would be sympathetic to the idea of ensuring that education as a whole combined the liberal, scientific, and technical approaches, and this applies to secondary and tertiary education as well as primary education. He accepts the view that universities are places where knowledge is imparted and research conducted, but he does not consider that to be the main reason for their existence. Teaching and research could be performed equally well and much more cheaply in other ways.

The justification for a university is that it preserves the connection between knowledge and the zest for life, by uniting the young and the old in the imaginative consideration of learning. The university imparts information, but it imparts it imaginatively. At least, this is the function which it should perform for society. A university which fails in this respect has no reason for existence.[44]

It should also promote, 'the imaginative acquisition of knowledge' for without imagination 'it is nothing—at least nothing useful'.[45] Gandhi's philosophy of education is basically in line with Whitehead's philosophy here, and whereas the former envisages the importance of establishing a link between universities and industry so that society as a whole might benefit, the latter refers pointedly to the need for the general functions of a university to incorporate the particular functions of a business school, the main purpose of which 'is to produce men with a greater zest for business'.[46] Both clearly have the welfare of society as a whole in mind when they seek to establish grounds for the justification for higher education.

Gandhi, as we have seen, draws no distinction between intellectual and vocational training; the one was not possible without the other. So he crosses the binary divide when he comments on higher education with the words: 'The university which I visualize will consist of masons, carpenters and weavers who will be truly intellectual social workers ...'[47] He makes another interesting point when he maintains that higher education should involve private enterprise, and that financial support from that quarter should apply equally to education in the arts as to technical and industrial education.[48] This means that he was not opposed to higher education *per se*, as some commentators would have us believe, but simply that it ought not to be supported from the general resources of the state. On the other hand, should the state have need of the services of people educated in certain types of subjects, then it should be prepared to pay for their education. In the main, however, universities should seek to be self-supporting.[49]

When those who were convinced that he was opposed to the provision of higher education asked him why he adopted such an attitude, his reply was that people were mistaken in assuming that he was opposed to it. In point of fact he favoured higher education for all who might benefit from it, but he did not believe it should be provided for the few at the expense of many tax-payers. Education needed a radical overhaul so that the life of a prospective graduate should not be totally divorced from the life of people in the villages.[50] It is in this connection also that he refers to the intellectual damage done to the people of India, and the moral injury inflicted upon them, by the alien system of education that had been imposed upon them by the British, and imparted through the medium of a foreign language. The insistence of the authorities that all education had to be through the medium of English, had done irreparable damage to Indian society by creating barriers within families, and making students strangers in their own homes. The wrong done to millions of his fellow-countrymen by this 'false de-Indianizing education' was beyond measure. How much easier it would have been if, in his case for example, Gujarati had been the medium of instruction; and was it not the case that the language of Gujarati would have been enriched in the process? Far from being the enemy of higher education as was being suggested, therefore, he was very much in favour of it, provided it was radically overhauled along the lines he indicated.[51] We shall examine his criticism of the use of English as the medium of instruction in schools, and his insistence on the benefits that would derive from the use of the vernacular in the educational programme, in greater detail in the following chapter.

Notes

1. *The Collected Works of Mahatma Gandhi* (hereafter, CWMG), Second Revised Edition, Ministry of Information and Broadcasting, Government of India, New Delhi, 1969–; Vol. 72, p. 380
2. CWMG, Vol. 72, pp. 378–81
3. Ibid., Vol.75, pp. 146–66
4. Ibid., Vol. 39, p. 416
5. Ibid., Vol. 52, p. 68
6. Ibid., Vol. 51, p. 402
7. Ibid., p. 348
8. CWMG, Vol. 68, pp. 338–43
9. Ibid., Vol. 40, p. 417
10. Ibid., Vol. 66, p. 194
11. Ibid., Vol. 41, pp. 173–5
12. Ibid., Vol. 41, p. 71
13. CWMG, Vol. 39, pp. 414–15
14. Ibid., Vol. 41, p. 71
15. Ibid., Vol. 75, pp.153–5
16. M.K. Gandhi, *All Men are Brothers*, edited by Krishna Kripalani, UNESCO, Paris, 1958, 1969, p. 151

17. Ibid., p. 157
18. Margaret Donaldson, *Children's Minds*, Collins, Glasgow, 1978, 1981, pp. 127–8
19. CWMG, Vol. 65, p. 235; Vol. 69, p. 203
20. Ibid., Vol. 66, pp. 32–3
21. Ibid., p. 169
22. N.K. Bose, *Selections from Gandhi*, Navajivan Trust, Ahmedabad, 1948, 1972, p. 52
23. *The Selected Works of Mahatma Gandhi*, Navajivan Trust, Ahmedabad, 1968, Vol. VI, p. 393
24. Ibid.
25. CWMG, Vol. 76, pp. 250–51
26. Ibid., Vol. 23, p. 239
27. Ibid., Vol. 24, p. 563
28. Sir Stewart Sutherland, *The Price of Ignorance*, Hume Occasional Paper No. 47, The David Hume Institute, Edinburgh, 1995
29. Ibid., p. 10
30. Ibid., p. 11
31. CWMG, Vol. 21, p. 39
32. *With Gandhiji in Ceylon*, p. 109, quoted in Iyer, *The Moral and Political Writings of Mahatma Gandhi*, Vol. 3, p. 382
33. CWMG, Vol. 19, p. 484
34. Ibid., Vol. 69, p. 205
35. Ibid., pp. 370–7
36. CWMG, Vol. 66, p. 218
37. Ibid., Vol. 73, p. 104
38. Ibid., Vol. 42, p. 404
39. *Selected Works*, Vol. VI, p. 521
40. *All Men are Brothers*, p. 153
41. *Selected Works*, Vol. VI, p. 526
42. *Selections from Gandhi*, pp. 284–5
43. Louis Fischer, *The Essential Gandhi*, Vintage Books, New York, 1962, pp. 236–7
44. A.N. Whitehead, *An Anthology*, selected by F.S.C. Northrop & Mason W. Gross, Cambridge University Press, Cambridge, 1953, p. 130
45. Ibid., p. 134
46. Ibid., p. 131
47. CWMG, Vol. 36, p. 422
48. Ibid., Vol. 66, p. 195
49. Ibid., Vol. 67, pp. 158–163
50. Ibid., Vol. 70, p. 304; Vol. 67, p. 159
51. Ibid., Vol. 67, pp. 158–163

chapter four

Education and *Swarāj*

An important aspect of Gandhi's philosophy of education is his view of the importance of the language used as the medium of instruction in schools and colleges. He insists that the use of English as the medium of instruction in the education of the youth of India had done incalculable damage to the nation both intellectually and morally. It meant that Indians had become 'dis-Indianized, without becoming Europeanized in the proper sense'.[1] It had broken the concordance that existed between home and school by undermining the importance of the mother tongue of those involved in the educational process. He argues that if education had been imparted through the vernacular rather than through a foreign tongue 'neighbours would have partaken of our knowledge'.[2] He recalls with misgiving his own school experience of the priority given to the mastery of English before learning could begin, and of the punishment inflicted on those caught speaking their mother tongue in class, in his case Gujarati. This policy it seems was the accepted English practice because it was not confined to India. A similar educational system was imposed on Wales in the nineteenth century, when English was made the medium of instruction in Welsh schools, and the use of the mother tongue discouraged by the infliction of mental and physical punishments. Those children who were caught speaking their native language in school were forced to wear around their necks a wooden token or note, known in Welsh circles as the 'Welsh not'. This usually passed from one pupil to another whenever an infringement of the English-only rule occurred and the offending mother tongue was spoken. The boy or girl who happened to be wearing the token at the end of the day was appropriately punished. Commenting on his first day in school, Owen Edwards wrote later in life that 'a string was placed around my neck with a heavy wooden block attached to it...I understood later that it was placed around my neck because I spoke Welsh ... I did not understand the principle involved, but my nature rebelled against such a devilish practice which destroyed the foundations of a child's character.'[3] In this kind of educational system, it did not matter if a child spoke bad English since bad English was preferable to good Welsh. Referring to this practice the point is made that it required a great deal of effort for a child who spoke only Welsh at home and at play, to enter school at the age of five to be instructed through the medium of English, and to be punished for resorting, even involuntarily, to the use of the familiar mother tongue. 'What suffered most in the crude process was native creative imaginative thinking; that began to gather rust and, as always, rust once established was very difficult to remove.'[4] The poet Idris Davies, as a result of this educational system, ceased to be a monoglot Welshman. The language of the hearth continued to be Welsh, but at play with his friends he came to rely more on English to convey his thoughts. What he came to regret in later life was the ability to write creatively in his mother tongue.

> 'I lost my native language
> For the one the Saxon spake
> By going to school to order
> For education's sake'[5]

It is difficult to fault Gandhi's argument that it would have been much easier for him to grasp the rudiments of subjects taught at school had he been able to learn them through the medium of his mother tongue. Furthermore, he correctly assumes that the vocabulary of Gujarati would have been enriched in the process by the acquisition of new terms if this policy had been applied.

If I had, instead, passed those precious seven years in mastering Gujarati and had learnt mathematics, science, and Sanskrit and other subjects through Gujarati, I could easily have shared the knowledge so gained with my neighbours. I would have enriched Gujarati, and who can say that I would not have with my habit of application and my inordinate love for the country and mother tongue, made a richer and greater contribution to the service of the masses?[6]

The school, he claims, ought to be a natural extension of the home, so that the impressions received at school might be in accordance with the impressions received at home, and that pupils might be allowed to build on their own cultural heritage. He is firmly of the view that real education for the people of India was impossible through the medium of a foreign language. It led to the neglect of the indigenous culture of the nation; it estranged students from their mother tongue; and it cut them off from their roots in the cultural traditions of their country.

In a speech delivered at Newlands Government School in South Africa, General Hertzog stressed the importance of the mother tongue in the education of children, and Gandhi makes the point that what was true for the Dutch children Hertzog was referring to, was equally true for Indian children. Indifference to the mother tongue, no matter how humble, meant that we were 'in danger of forgetting a universal religious principle', involving self-identity and national identity. It was impossible 'to exist as independent, self-respecting human beings if we forget the poetry of the race to which we belong'.[7] In Gandhi's view, the only reason why Indians were not totally alienated from their cultural heritage, which was often depicted as barbarous and superstitious, was because they were too firmly rooted in the ancient traditions of their country.[8] So the sooner the educated people of India freed themselves from what he calls the hypnotic spell of a foreign medium the better it would be for India as a whole. Was it really necessary, he asks, to acquire an English education before speaking about home rule? Europeans had discarded the practice that appeared to be in vogue in India. For example, great efforts were being made 'to revive a knowledge of Welsh among Welshmen', and Wales was simply 'a small portion of England' and its language 'no language at all'. Was it not then 'a sad commentary' that Indians 'should have to speak of Home Rule in a foreign tongue'?[9] These comments on Wales and its language would hardly have met with the approval of ardent Welshmen, who are naturally as proud of their cultural heritage, and the literary wealth of their nation, as Gandhi was of the cultural heritage of India. Doubtless, greater knowledge of the language and culture of this so-called small part of England would have forced him to revise his opinion, and at the same time to recognize the close comparisons that could be drawn between Wales and India as a result of the imposition of an alien system of education. But his ignorance of what had happened in Wales does not detract from the point he was making, namely, that the alien education system imposed on India fostered what he called 'the tyranny of English', which ignored and undermined the importance of the mother tongue of the people involved in the educational process. He argued, with some justification, that it created a barrier between the pupils themselves and members of their own family. He makes the point, for example, that his father was an intelligent man who spoke his mother tongue fluently, but he had no knowledge of English, and consequently was not able to understand what his son was studying at school. The inevitable result of all this was that Gandhi came to feel a stranger in his own home, alienated from his kith and kin, and in some ways superior to them. But his indictment of the English educational system was not simply that it had inflicted a moral and intellectual injury on the Indian nation, by undermining its literary foundations, and damaging its cultural heritage, but that it was also a violation of Truth, an affront to Indian self-respect, and a grievous blow to the self-identity and national identity of the Indian people.

Commenting on the need for a radical change in the provision of national education in India he argues that instruction in schools should be given through the medium of the mother tongue. He fails to understand why English should be used as the medium of instruction in India, when other nations are able to employ their own languages.[10] In a letter to Rabindranath Tagore in which he was eliciting the latter's opinion on the subject, he poses the question whether Hindi should not be made a compulsory second language in all post-primary schools, and whether the teaching in all schools and colleges should not be through the vernacular.[11]

Giving evidence before the Disorders Inquiry Committee, on 9 January 1920, under the presidency of Lord Hunter, Gandhi commented on the unsoundness of the educational system in India. Arguing that it had conspicuously failed to produce balanced individuals, he pointed out two major defects in the programme. The first was the lack of any moral or religious education in the schools, and the second was that the use of English as the medium of instruction placed 'such a strain upon the intellectual resources of the youths who are receiving the education, they really do not assimilate the noblest ideas that are imparted to them through the schools. They have got nothing but parrot's training, the very best of them.'[12] In a similar vein, in a speech delivered at the Sind National College, on 24 July 1920, he refers to the burden of English being so heavy for Indian students that it crushed all original thinking, which was the primary reason in his view why Hindi should become the language of the whole of India.[13]

He was at the forefront in promoting the cause of the vernacular as the medium of instruction in the educational system of India. He failed to see why English should be accepted as the *lingua franca* of education, and insisted that there was a strong case to be made for Hindi as the medium of instruction in secondary schools and universities since it suited almost all the provinces of India.[14] He goes further when he maintains that national education would be incomplete without the use of Hindi as the medium of instruction.[15] There could be no *swarāj*, in his view, without people being freed from the tyranny of English, and pride being restored in the indigenous languages of Sanskrit and Hindi.[16]

In response to questions posed by two barristers on board the ship *Gurkha* on the subject of education, Gandhi claims that the use of a foreign medium of instruction in schools had succeeded in destroying the creative and imaginative faculties of students and in making them unworthy trustees of the nation's culture.[17] His convocation address at the Bihar Vidyapith, Patna, on 30 January 1927, follows similar lines when he claims that 'as a result of English being the medium of instruction, we have lost all originality'.[18] The policy of displacing the vernacular in favour of English was nothing but a tragedy, for it had created a generation of crammers and imitators unfit for original work. Furthermore it had made the children of India foreigners in their own land.[19] He observes: 'Of all the superstitions that affect India, none is so great as that a knowledge of the English language is necessary for imbibing ideas of liberty and developing accuracy of thought.'[20] The whole system of education in India in his view had been conceived in error and nurtured in sin.[21] The canker had eaten so deep into Indian society that many considered knowledge of English to be the whole purpose of education while for him it was a sign of slavery and degradation. These are strong words for Gandhi to use in reference to what he conceived to be the iniquity of an English-oriented education. But it did not mean that he was totally opposed to the use of the English language in all circumstances in India. On the contrary, he supports efforts to acquire a mastery of English and other languages, but not to the neglect or exclusion of the native languages. 'I would not have a single Indian to forget, neglect or be ashamed of his mother tongue,' he says, 'or to feel that he or she cannot think or express, the best thoughts in his or her own vernacular.'[22]

He refers to what he calls the curse of the use of a foreign medium of instruction in schools: 'Among the many evils of foreign rule this blighting imposition of a foreign medium upon the youth of the country will be counted by history as one of the greatest. It has sapped the energy of the nation, it has shortened the lives of the pupils, it has estranged them from the masses, it has made education unnecessarily expensive. If this process is still persisted in, it bids fair to rob the nation of its soul. The sooner therefore educated India shakes itself free from the hypnotic spell of the foreign medium, the better it would be for them and the people.'[23] The nation is robbed of its soul, in Gandhi's view, when it fails to acquire knowledge of the Self, the *Ātman*, which is the primary aim of education. This knowledge is arrived at, not by the study of English literature and culture, but through an understanding of the religious and cultural traditions of the Hindu way of life. Respect for Sanskrit and the indigenous languages of India, together with its literary heritage might well be considered the necessary prerequisites for such an understanding.

The burden involved in acquiring a knowledge of English, in Gandhi's view, meant that students spent eleven years pursuing a course that could be completed in seven through the medium of the vernacular. His own experience up to the age of twelve was that everything would have been much easier for him if Gujarati had been used as the medium of instruction. He recalls with misgiving his days at the high school, when he spent half his time seeking to master English before proceeding to study science and art subjects, all of which were taught through the medium of English.[24] In any event he was convinced that children got nothing more in high schools than 'a half-baked knowledge of English'.[25] Furthermore the use of English only created barriers within the family unit, making children strangers in their own homes. The study of literature in schools under the British educational system consisted of the appreciation of English prose and poetry, and Gandhi makes the point that if he had spent his time mastering Gujarati, rather than English language and literature, his mother tongue would have been greatly enriched. Immeasurable damage had been done to millions in India by the imposition of a 'false de-Indianizing education',[26] which had maimed people mentally.[27] Furthermore, the indigenous languages of India had been greatly impoverished by the hypnotic spell English exercised over the people. Even Congressmen insisted on speaking it, and unfortunately compelled others to do the same. In Gandhi's view, it was difficult to measure the disservice done to India by this wanton neglect of her native languages.[28] Infatuation with English had resulted in unfaithfulness to the provincial languages,[29] loss of originality,[30] and diminution of the mind and spirit of the Indian people.[31]

By stressing the need for the proper use of provincial languages in the educational system of the country Gandhi was concerned, as we have seen, not only with preserving the soul of the nation, and restoring the self-respect of his fellow-countrymen, but also with the fundamental question of self-identity. Kant, as we have noted, regards the purpose of education as being concerned with our very identity as human beings and enabling man to be fully human. It follows that without it we suffer a lack of self-knowledge, and to an extent are dehumanized. Gandhi's view would be that without a proper educational system India was in danger of losing its soul.

If we were to examine this question further from a philosophical point of view, we could say that in order for a person to know who he is, he must know himself as someone who occupies space, shows certain characteristics of appearance and behaviour, and be able to distinguish himself from his neighbours, or from people similar to himself. It follows from this that the basis of our knowledge of another person is that he also is an occupant of space with whom we can communicate by means of language, and the presupposition of language is that statements are means of communication which bind us together. We know ourselves, therefore, as members of a human community bound together by language. The implication of this view is that the nature of that language, together with its literature, culture and institutions, will directly affect and influence our identity. A person is rooted in a human community which is bound together by language. It is the community which makes it possible for the life of that individual to be meaningful, and which gives him a sense of identity.

On the basis of this analysis it is possible to say that the people of India know themselves as members of a community which shares the same cultural heritage, the same languages, and the same traditions. This may be bound up with what Simone Weil calls the 'need for roots' and what we have here referred to as self-identity. What needs to be asked is whether it is possible for an individual to retain a true sense of self-identity if the culture and traditions of the community in which he lives, and the language which binds him to his neighbours, are undermined by the imposition of an alien language and culture introduced by means of an educational system which is profoundly divisive in its effects.

Gandhi would not quarrel with the conclusion arrived at concerning the significance of the cultural heritage and language of the community to which one belongs, or the importance of an awareness of a dimension of the past. His concern with self-knowledge and self-identity was related to the knowledge of Truth, and any violation of the self is a violation of Truth. His indictment of the alien educational system that fostered what he calls 'the tyranny of English' is that it inflicted a moral and intellectual injury on India. It undermined the foundation, and damaged the fabric of the nation, by ignoring the languages, and neglecting the culture, that bound various communities together. With a certain amount of justification he is able to refer to 'the enormity of the damage done' and 'the incalculable intellectual and moral injury' sustained by the nation as a result of the educational policy of the British Raj. It was his firm conviction that it was impossible for the people of India to be truly educated through the medium of a foreign language, and to the complete exclusion of the native, indigenous culture. It meant that they were cut off from their roots, that children were estranged from their parents, and that they were alienated from their cultural milieu.[32] Therefore, among the many methodological changes suggested by Gandhi for the educational system of India is the need to recognize the importance of the use of the vernacular as the medium of instruction in schools.

This was the basis of *swarāj*. There could be no self-rule without freedom from the hypnotic spell of English.[33] There could be no self-respect without a deep awareness of the cultural heritage of the nation. There could be no sense of self-identity without an awareness of having roots in a community that shared the same religious and cultural traditions. There could be no *swarāj* without self-reliance, and the symbol of self-belief and self-reliance was the spinning-wheel. Far from being the abnegation of progress through industrialization, as Arthur Koestler would have us believe,[34] it was, in Gandhi's view, the symbol of self-determination. Koestler was mistaken in his belief that the charkha was a symbol of the rejection of industrialization. On the contrary it was the symbol of self-respect, self-help, self-belief, and self-reliance, and its daily use symbolized India's desire for self-determination and *swarāj*. It symbolized a more acceptable, decentralized form of industrialization where people mattered, and where power was not concentrated in the hands of the few who amassed fortunes at the expense of the many.[35] National education would be inadequate and incomplete without Hindi, rather than English, as the medium of instruction in schools; it would also suffer without the spinning-wheel as the symbol of self-reliance. Under *swarāj* the spinning-wheel would provide the necessary resources for the introduction of a constructive educational programme in India.[36]

The fundamental need, however, was for self-development, self-fulfilment, and the cultivation of an awareness of one's own identity. There could be no *swarāj* without knowledge of the *Ātman*, and this was the ultimate goal of education.

Notes

1. *The Collected Works of Mahatma Gandhi* (hereafter, CWMG), Second Revised Edition, Ministry of Information and Broadcasting, Government of India, New Delhi, 1969–, Vol. 12, p. 371.
2. CWMG, Vol 13, p. 221
3. Owen Edwards, *Clych Atgof: Penodau yn hanes fy Addysg*, Cwmni Cyhoeddwyr Cymreig, Caernarfon, 1906, pp. 15–6
4. Islwyn Jenkins, *Idris Davies of Rhymney*, Gomer Press, Llandysul, 1986, p. 35
5. Ibid.
6. CWMG, Vol. 67, pp. 159–161; cf. M.K. Gandhi, *All Men are Brothers*, edited by Krishna Kripalani, UNESCO, Paris, 1958, 1969, pp. 153–4
7. Ibid., Vol. 11, p. 146.
8. N.K. Bose, *Selections from Gandhi*, Navajivan Trust, Ahmedabad, 1948, 1972, pp. 283–4
9. CWMG, Vol. 10, p. 55
10. Ibid., Vol. 14, pp. 37–42
11. Ibid., p. 163
12. Ibid., Vol. 16, p. 450. Compare the condensed version in *Young India*, 21, 28 January 1920
13. Ibid., Vol. 18, p. 85
14. Ibid., Vol. 17, p. 335

15. Ibid., Vol. 19, p. 481
16. Ibid., Vol. 13, pp. 358–9
17. Ibid., Vol. 19, p. 133
18. Ibid., Vol. 33, p. 27
19. Ibid., Vol. 21, pp. 39–40
20. Ibid., Vol 20, pp. 42–3
21. Ibid.
22. Ibid., Vol. 20, p. 159
23. Ibid., Vol. 37, p. 22
24. *Selected Works*, Vol. VI, p. 510
25. CWMG, Vol. 66, pp. 117–8
26. Ibid., Vol. 67, pp. 159–161
27. Ibid., p. 194
28. Ibid., Vol. 75, pp. 156–7
29. Ibid., Vol. 72, p. 380
30. Ibid., Vol. 33, pp. 26–7
31. Ibid., Vol. 20, p. 43
32. *Selections from Gandhi*, p. 284
33. CWMG, Vol 13, p. 359
34. Arthur Koestler, 'The Yogi and the Commissar', *New York Times Magazine*, 5 October, 1969
35. *Selections from Gandhi*, p. 71
36. CWMG, Vol. 19, pp. 481, 484

chapter five

Education and Religion

The primary aim of education for Gandhi, as for Plato, is the nurture of the soul, the *Ātman*. In his view, it is imperative that education promote self-knowledge and self-fulfilment, the development of character, and the cultivation of the whole man, body, mind, and spirit. In the final analysis this is the kind of education that will lead to the uplift of society as a whole. He is convinced that education without 'lofty conduct and morality' is dangerous, and that society will only benefit from it 'provided that, along with it, people acquired truthful conduct and moral life'.[1] His considered view is that if education were not to be used for the public good, then it could very well act like poison in the body politic.[2] What this means, so far as Gandhi is concerned, is that education has to be religiously and ethically oriented; it has to aim at enabling people to live a life that is spiritually uplifting, and intrinsically worthwhile. So its primary objective, from his standpoint, goes a step beyond the view of those who insist that education should be pursued for its own sake, or that it is in itself inherently valuable. It also transcends the limited, utilitarian view of those who believe that education should always serve a useful purpose, that it should be concerned solely with vocational training, that its main aim should be to prepare students for an occupation in life, and that it should enable them to earn a living, maintain a family, and make a satisfactory contribution to society. It could be argued, however, that introducing students to a way of life that is intrinsically worthwhile, should involve recognizing both the inherent value of education as a means of promoting an understanding of the meaning and significance of life, and also the importance of acquiring the skills and abilities necessary to enable them to fulfil the demands of a vocation. That is, it could be maintained that education should be vocationally oriented on the one hand, and on the other, promote an understanding of the meaning of life. So, informed, practical knowledge, and an understanding of the principles that relate to the ultimate purpose of life, could well be considered to be the necessary prerequisites of true education.

Yet if, as we have shown, the development of the whole man, body, mind, and spirit, is what Gandhi's conceives the aim of true education to be, then it has to be conceded that it involves recognizing the importance of the religious dimension in the educational process. This corresponds to Whitehead's view that the essence of education is that it should be religious.[3] It follows that, from Gandhi's point of view, education should be concerned not just with training a person for a vocation, or concentrating on a narrow specialism, or promoting the acquisition of informed knowledge, valuable as those goals might be, but recognizing also that it is a process whereby a person's outlook is transformed, the quality of his life enhanced, and his understanding of the meaning and significance of life deepened. So true education, for Gandhi, involves both breadth and depth: it combines both knowledge and understanding. And when breadth and depth are combined in the process of educating the whole person, what is effected is self-realization, the promotion of understanding, and the preservation of social values. That is, the principles of autonomy and heteronomy are harmonized. The individual, when he pursues his quest for an understanding of the true nature of the self, does so in accordance with traditional values, and within the framework of what is socially uplifting. Self-realization and social amelioration go hand in hand; the one is not pursued in isolation from the other. Or as Gandhi would put it: realizing the true nature of the Self, the Ātman, involves sarvodaya, the uplift of humanity as a whole. If we enquire what it is that would bring about the uplift of society, and make life intrinsically worthwhile for everyone, the clear aim of a religiously oriented education, it could be said that it would doubtless involve cultivating the capacity to think, promoting consistency and clarity of thought, freeing the mind from prejudices, eliminating erroneous presuppositions and ideas, and above all, from Gandhi's viewpoint, establishing the nature of Truth. To know the Truth, for him, is to know the true nature of the self, which is akin to knowing God, and the nature of the ultimate reality.

It is the claim of many educationists today that we acquire greater depth of understanding and breadth of vision by pursuing the values implicit in the use of reason. Gandhi would not disagree with this claim, but he would insist at the same time that true education has to be religiously oriented as well as rationally inspired. So the educated person is one who, while pursuing the goals implicit in the use of reason in seeking to live a life that is intrinsically worthwhile, and while including breadth of vision, also seeks depth of understanding in order to apprehend the true nature of the self.

The primary purpose of education for Gandhi is to know the Self, the *Ātman*, which is synonymous with knowing God, *Sat*, or Truth, *Satya*. This in turn points to the integral relationship that he conceives to exist between a religious orientation and self-realization. Real education is character-building, not literacy.[4] It does not consist in accumulating facts and figures, or reading many books, or passing examinations; rather it consists in developing character.[5] It is the education of the heart rather than the head.[6] It is not the packing of unwanted information into the heads of students, thereby crushing originality and producing automata.[7] It is spiritual development rather than the study of English or literature, or acquiring the ability to earn a livelihood.[8] It would be degrading in the extreme if earning a livelihood were to be regarded as the sole aim of education, since its primary goal is *mokṣa*, the liberation of the soul.[9] It is concerned, therefore, with the development of the whole man, body, mind, and spirit. The nurture of the soul had been ignored in the past, and even the cultivation of man's skills and abilities had been atrophied in the national system of education. So it was high time for these defects to be remedied: 'I would develop in the child his hands, his brain and his soul. The hands have almost atrophied. The soul has been altogether ignored. I therefore put in a plea in season and out of season for correcting these grave defects in our education.'[10]

So true knowledge and true education, must involve knowing the Self, the *Ātman*, which, in Gandhi's view, is the only thing worth knowing.[11] It means recognizing the relationship that exists between the true self and God, in order that we might understand the meaning of the quest for Truth, and be delivered 'from darkness, sensuous pleasure and capricious behaviour'.[12] It means living our lives and fashioning our conduct in the light of that knowledge,[13] and learning to live the good life.[14] Education is that which draws out the very best that is in us, and it would be of little use if we did not 'learn the art of feeling one with the poorest in the land'.[15] Education should develop the body, mind and spirit, since 'Man is neither intellect nor the gross animal body, nor the heart or soul alone. A proper and harmonious combination of all three is required for the making of the whole man...'.[16] Education should reveal above all the qualities of the spirit, and in the final analysis lead to *mokṣa*, liberation.[17] It should promote man's spiritual development[18] and cultivate character side by side with the pursuit of literature.[19] It should evoke and develop a student's talents enabling him to come to terms with the basic problems of life.[20] So, for Gandhi, the emphasis is as much on the spiritual as on the practical aspects of education, and he insists that it would be a mistake to seek to cultivate the mind in isolation from the body and the spirit. Referring to the Gujarati word for education, *kelavani*, he points out that it has the same connotation as the English term 'education', namely, 'drawing out'; it implies the development of latent talents, or as Plato would describe it, the cultivation of the inherent qualities of the soul. The Welsh word for culture, *diwylliant*, has a similar connotation; its literal meaning is 'to make less wild', and its purpose is the removal of all those harmful tendencies that prevent the cultivation of man's latent, beneficent qualities. True education, for Gandhi as for Plato, is that which cultivates the soul or the spirit, and which leads ultimately to the complete development of the whole man.

Gandhi's stress on the importance of self-realization, or knowing the true nature of the *Ātman*, and God, or Truth, prompts us to look again at his indebtedness to the religious tradition in which he was nurtured. As we have shown, to be able to understand his general philosophy, and his educational theories in particular, we need some kind of appreciation of what he means by Truth. His followers in India believed his concept of Truth was linked to the Hindu concepts of *dharma* and *ṛta*, that is, the concepts of duty and the moral law. So it can be said that his experiments with Truth are ultimately determined by his understanding of the Hindu tradition.

To a great extent, as we have shown, Gandhi was an Advaitin in the classical mould, and can be said to have derived his views about the nature of the self, *Ātman*, and its relation to Truth and *Brahman*, from the religious tradition in which he was nurtured. It is possible, as we have seen, to point to similarities and differences between his position and that of Sankara. In many ways, however, his thought bears a closer resemblance to the teaching of the Hindu reformer, Vivekananda. He certainly echoes the teaching of the latter when he claims that there as many religions as there are individuals, and that even within particular, historical religions there are different viewpoints manifesting different facets of the truth.[21] Again, they both distinguish between personal and impersonal conceptions of God, and the highest concept of the divine, for Vivekananda, is the Vedāntic concept of Being, Consciousness, Bliss. The essence of religion, for him, is to see God as 'the Soul of our souls, the Reality in us'.[22] All that exists is in effect a manifestation of Being itself which is the impersonal God, the One through whom we know, see, think and exist: 'He is the essence of our own Self. He is the essence of this ego, this I and we cannot know anything excepting in and through that I. Therefore you have to know everything in and through Brahman.'[23] The impersonal God is the only reality for Vivekananda. All else is unreal and manifested by the power of *māyā*. *Brahman* is Truth, and the Self of man. The purpose of life is to know the Truth, and we attain knowledge of Truth when we come to know that we are at one with the Universal Being.[24]

Like Vivekananda, Gandhi expresses a preference for the impersonal concept of God, and his claim that Truth and Reality are one, corresponds to Vivekananda's view that the impersonal God is Being itself. But comparisons between the two go even further. As Gandhi refers to personifications of the ultimate as an indication of man's desire for symbols, so Vivekananda refers to forms and images as symbols manifesting man's attempt to realize the ultimate.

The Hindus have discovered that the absolute can only be realized, or thought of, or stated, through the relative, and the images, crosses, and crescents are simply so many symbols—so many pegs to hang spiritual ideas on. It is not that this help is necessary for everyone, but those that do need it have no right to say that it is wrong.[25]

Gandhi's reference to symbols as manifestations of man's craving for the unseen and intangible, corresponds to Vivekananda's claim that they are pegs for spiritual ideas. Both recognize the need for symbolic representations of the ultimate, and both maintain that they are necessary for the religious life of many people. Both agree that image worship is an indication of man's need for symbols, and ought not to be construed as idol worship. Both express a preference for the impersonal concept of God as Being itself or Truth, and both would agree that there is nothing wrong in conceiving God in personal terms. Gandhi, however, draws no distinction between the two concepts. It makes no difference to him whether God is conceived in one way or the other, since, for him, the personal concept of God is not inferior to the impersonal concept. His readiness to acknowledge that God is all things to all men enables his to accept the validity of the *Dvaita* and *Viśiṣṭādvaita* positions, while at the same time maintaining his preference for *Advaita*. Vivekananda, on the other hand, sees the concept of a personal God as characteristic of the religion of the masses. He recognizes that those who do not need such a concept have no right to condemn it, and he acknowledges that it has its rightful place in the social structure. Nevertheless, in his view, it represents an inferior position and a lower form of truth. His claim is that *Dvaita* is fulfilled by *Viśiṣṭādvaita*, which in turn finds complete fulfilment in *Advaita*.

Now, as society exists at the present time, all these three stages are necessary; the one does not deny the other, one is simply the fulfilment of the other. The Advaitist or qualified Advaitist does not say that dualism is wrong; it is a right view, but a lower one. It is on the way to truth; therefore let everybody work out his own vision of this universe, according to his own ideas.[26]

If Gandhi is at odds with Vivekānanda on the question of the superiority of the *Advaita* position, he is at one with him on the question of the unity of existence which, according to Vivekananda, is the main lesson man needs to learn.[27] The difference between man and the animal kingdom is one of degree and not kind, for man is at one with the universe.[28] The test of spirituality is the ability to recognize the oneness of life, and this occurs when the veil of ignorance falls from man's eyes and he achieves the state of *jivan-mukti*, or self-liberation.[29] He sees that there is but one Self, one reality, and that the empirical world is a manifestation of the One.[30] The unity of the individual self with the universal Self means that an individual cannot inflict an injury on another without injuring himself. So *ahiṁsā*, for Vivekananda, as for Gandhi, is the inescapable corollary of belief in the essential unity of mankind.

'Thou art with this Universal Being, and, as such, every soul that exists is your soul; and every body that exists is your body; and in hurting anyone, you hurt yourself, in loving anyone, you love yourself.'[31]

The similarities between the views of Gandhi and Vivekananda on the question of the non-violent implications of the unity of mankind are evident. The same is true of the social implications of the doctrine, as we indicated, when similarities between *sarvodaya* and the views of some of the proponents of liberation theology were examined.

The similarity between Gandhi's view of religion and that of Vivekananda is also evident. For the latter religion is in essence one, and its goal is the realization of God in the soul.[32] Nevertheless it takes different forms in accordance with the various circumstances of people. So far as externals are concerned there may be as many sects or religions as there are human beings. Truth can be expressed in a variety of different ways embodying different philosophies, mythologies and rituals, but in essence it is one. The ideal universal religion is that which produces a harmonious balance of the elements of philosophy, mysticism and emotion. 'And this religion is attained by what we... call Yoga-union. To the worker, it is union between men and the whole of humanity; to the mystic, between his lower and Higher Self; to the lover, union between himself and the God of Love; and to the philosopher, it is union of all existence.'[33]

Gandhi speaks of religion as one which becomes many as it passes through the human medium. Religions for him, as for Vivekānanda, correspond to the variety of environments and temperaments that exist in the world. There are as many religions as there are individuals but they are simply different roads leading to the same goal. Religion is that which underlies all religions; it harmonizes them and gives them reality; it is that element in human nature which seeks to realise the oneness of the Soul and Truth, or God.[34]

The similarities between Gandhi's views and the views of Vivekananda are sufficiently clear to enable us to say that he is closer to the neo-Vedāntic position in some respects than to classical Vedānta, and that the similarities between them extend well beyond the concept of the essential oneness of existence. While differences between them exist, it is still evident that Gandhi is in tune with Vivekananda's basic position, and with the way the latter develops the moral, social and political implications of his metaphysical beliefs. For that reason he is, like Vivekananda, a reformer in the modern Hindu tradition. What we can conclude from this analysis is that his indebtedness to the religious tradition in which he was nurtured was significant, and that any understanding of his general philosophical position, and his educational theories in particular, requires an appreciation of that tradition.

It is as a self-professed Advaitin then that Gandhi equates knowing the Self, the Ātman, with knowing the true nature of Reality, Sat, and with knowing God, or Truth, Satya. For him self-realization is God-realization, which in turn is the realization of Truth. This raises the interesting question whether he saw the need to establish a place for religious studies in the school curriculum. If true education consists in knowing the Self, the Ātman,[35] and knowing the relation that exists between the Self, God and Truth,[36] and if it leads also to the provision of depth of understanding and breadth of vision, then religious studies would appear to be the necessary prerequisite of his educational programme. It is significant that he considers education without religious instruction to be fruitless. This clearly accords with what he has to say about the importance of education being ethically oriented. Yet it is equally significant that he believes children should be provided with a secular as well as a religious education.

'We believe that the education of any people is fruitless without religious instruction. Therefore, it is the duty of parents with a religious bent of mind to provide their children with both religious and secular education.'[37]

It is worthy of note also, that the type of religious instruction he favours for schools is one that is open to the study of religions other than one's own. He is wholeheartedly supportive of an open-ended approach to the teaching of religion, and is favourably disposed to what is referred to today as religious pluralism. He commends the teaching of ethics and the main tenets of faiths other than his own, for example, because, as he claims, understanding and appreciating the different beliefs and doctrines of the great religions of the world in a spirit of reverence and tolerance can lead to a better appreciation of one's own faith.

A curriculum of religious instruction should include a study of the tenets of faiths other than one's own. For this purpose the students should be trained to cultivate the habit of understanding and appreciating the doctrines of various great religions of the world in a spirit of reverence and broad-minded tolerance. This, if properly done, would help to give them a spiritual assurance and a better appreciation of their own religion.[38]

Not for Gandhi, therefore, the narrow, exclusivist, dogmatic approach to religious education, or what he calls the religion of the prison house. He has no desire to confine religious education to instruction in the principles of the Hindu faith any more than he wishes the teaching of literature to be confined to the cultural heritage of India. In this respect he claims an affinity with other reformers, like Rammohan Roy and Rabindranath Tagore, who wanted the windows of India to be opened wide to the winds of culture from other lands, while seeking to ensure at the same time that there should be no neglect of its own culture.[39]

We have shown that his understanding of Truth is something he acquired within his own form of life, and that his experiments with Truth are ultimately determined by his understanding of the Hindu tradition. This is not to say, as we have suggested, that insights from other religious traditions do not also inform his apprehension of Truth. He acknowledges his debt to John Ruskin, for example, and especially to the views expressed in the latter's book, *Unto this Last*. In a speech delivered on 28 March 1932, 'Some reflections on education', he comments on Ruskin's advocacy of real education by insisting that:

Anybody who does not love truth and cannot recognize goodness or beauty lives in his own self-conceit and remains ignorant of spiritual joy. Similarly, he who has no hope, who has, in other word, no faith in divine justice, will never be cheerful in heart. And he who is without love, that is, lacks the spirit of ahimsa, who cannot look upon all living things as his kith and kin, will never know the secret of living.[40]

In Gandhi's view, Ruskin succeeded admirably in developing these ideas at length in his work, and they were in accord with his own views on education.

Gandhi was aware that some people believed only secular instruction should be given in schools, but he expressed a contrary view in reply to a question put to him on one occasion by a missionary. The latter claimed that very few Indians had much knowledge of their own religion, and that they were even ignorant of the *Bhagavad Gita*, the spiritual classic of Hinduism. In his reply Gandhi acknowledges that in a country like India, where most of the religions of the world were represented, and where so many denominations of the same religion abounded, there were difficulties in making provision for religious education. Nevertheless, he maintains that 'if India is not to declare spiritual bankruptcy, religious instruction of its youth must be held to be at least as necessary as secular instruction.'[41] In pursuit of this goal he outlines a system of religious education for schools which is very modern in its approach, and basically empathetic and pluralistic. He maintains, for example, that the curriculum of religious instruction should include not only a study of the tenets of faiths other than his own, but that the rule governing our approach should always be that the religions concerned are studied empathetically, and through the writings of known adherents.[42] This attitude would at least ensure that the tenets of a particular faith were expressed by protagonists rather than those who were antagonistic or prejudiced. It would ensure also that the study of religion was placed on the same footing as that of culture. Furthermore, there was no reason to assume that this empathetic, pluralistic, approach to the study of religion would necessarily weaken the faith of adherents in the tenets of their own religion. On the contrary, there was every reason to suppose that faith in one's own religion would be strengthened in the process. The preservation of one's own religion did not mean that we had to show contempt for other religions.[43]

This avant garde approach to religious education means that Gandhi can be compared with many contemporary writers who favour a pluralistic approach to the study of religions. Ninian Smart seems to be expressing similar views in his Heslington lectures, delivered at the University of York in 1966, which were concerned with the logic of religion and the requirements of a secular society. He argues that the doctrinal, mythical and ethical dimensions of religion belong to what he calls the realm of the parahistorical, while the ritual, experiential, and social dimensions fall within the historical sphere. A sound appreciation of religion demands that the parahistorical dimension should not be divorced from the historical approach, and that the study of religion should include both.[44] But the inner logic of religious studies drives us towards the comparative study of religion, and it follows that the narrow, dogmatic, restricted, approach is inadequate[45] Theology has to adopt 'the sympathetic appreciation of positions and faiths other than its own' and 'must be open, not closed'.[46] Smart echoes Gandhi in this respect, and especially when he insists that it is one thing to present a faith sympathetically but openly (that is, by showing an appreciation of the alternatives to it); it is quite another thing to teach people that it is true while remaining silent or prejudiced about alternatives.'[47] They seem to be expressing similar views also when, as

Smart points out, real commitment does not preclude sympathy for other religious viewpoints, nor is it made less secure in itself.[48]

The dialogical approach adopted by John Hick was prompted, in the first instance, by his encounter with different cultures and faiths while teaching at the University of Birmingham in England. He echoes the views of Ernst Troeltsch when he maintains that it is possible to experience divine revelation beyond the boundaries of Christianity and in different cultural contexts. He refers to religion as a universal dimension of human life, and its history from primitive forms to the status of world faiths as indicative of God's revelation. Man's response to this revelation has, in each case, been determined by the characteristics of his cultural tradition as is evident in Islam, Hinduism, Buddhism and Christianity.[49] Hick's position is that we need to recognize that God has many names and can be worshipped in many different ways, and that to a great extent our religious affiliation depends on our place of birth. While it is right to insist that the revelation of God in Christ should be proclaimed, it is equally right and proper to recognize other manifestations of the divine in the prophets, in Mohammed, and in the Buddha. What is needed is a change of attitude from confessionalism to a quest for truth; from exclusivism to dialogue.[50] It is imperative, Hick maintains, that we see God at work in the whole religious life of mankind; that we recognize different religions have different names for God; and that we accept men may encounter God under different images and symbols in different cultures and faiths.[51] Gandhi would have approved of this open-ended, pluralistic, and dialogical approach to the study of religion, simply because he deplored the narrow, exclusivist, dogmatic approach, which he refers to as the religion of the prison house. Religious education, in his view, should not be restricted to instruction in the principles of the Hindu faith any more than the teaching of literature should be confined to the cultural heritage of India.

Gandhi would have approved also of the views of Raimundo Panikkar for whom faith in the truth is paramount. The latter makes the point that for the Christian, God is the truth, while for the Buddhist, no-God is the truth. 'Both have *faith* in the truth', Panikkar maintains, 'but for one this faith expresses itself in the *belief* that "God exists", while for the other it expresses itself in the contrary proposition that, "God does not exist".'[52] Panikkar's presupposition is that faith in the truth is the same in all religious traditions, though expressions of belief may differ. Gandhi, as we have seen, refers to God in the Buddhist context as *dharma*, and given his experiments with truth, and his belief that self-realization is God-realization, which in turn is the realization of truth, it can be seen that he is not far removed from Panikkar's position. He is in total agreement with Panikkar when the latter insists that the rules that should apply in religious dialogue are: freedom from apologetics, commitment to truth, and recognition of the importance of the historical dimension, and the social and cultural milieux of religious traditions.[53] He would approve of Panikkar's view also, that any interpretation we might make of a religious tradition other than our own, ought to be at one with the interpretation offered by adherents of that tradition. To speak of image-worship as idol-worship in a pejorative sense, for example, without seeking the views of the worshippers themselves, is to introduce alien categories of understanding into a particular religious tradition. We have to recognize 'that there are no immutable categories that can serve as absolute criteria for judging everything under the sun'.[54] This is similar to the point made by Peter Winch, that in order to understand another way of life, the onus is on us to extend our understanding, rather than insisting on seeing everything in terms of our ready-made distinctions between what is rational or irrational, right or wrong, true or false.[55] The principle of homogeneity is one that both Gandhi and Panikkar accept, because both believe that religious concepts can only be properly understood empathetically from within the religious and cultural traditions concerned, and from the standpoint of adherents of those traditions.

Gandhi's stress on the need for an empathetic approach to the study of religion means that he would be disposed to accept the inclusive attitude of Ernst Troeltsch, who was very much aware that religious and ethical ideas were subject to historical development and capable of great diversity. Troeltsch, for instance, rejects the attempt to guarantee the truth of Christianity on the grounds that it is the most perfect expression of religion and, in the Hegelian sense, the culmination of the universal process of the unfolding of the divine spirit. He argues rather, that the study of the history of religions does not point to an upward trend culminating in Christianity as the most perfect expression of religion, but rather that Christianity is simply one of the many forms in which the Divine Reason seeks to manifest itself.[56] Like Gandhi, he accepts the view that there is an element of truth in all religions, and views with disquiet those theological works which refer to the essence of religion as some kind of principle or power underlying all particular religions, and Christianity as the absolute realization of that essence. Such theological works subordinate historical investigation in the modern sense to the concept of a universal principle which is elevated to the status of a norm. Our knowledge of the history of religions, he claims, compels us to believe that it is not possible to speak of the essence of religion in such a way as to include the concept of a normative principle on the one hand and a graduated manifestation of that principle on the other. Furthermore, the modern study of history gives no indication that there is a progressive development from lower to higher forms of religious life culminating in Christianity. The higher religions are not related to one another in this way; rather, they stand in a parallel relationship to one another.[57] At no time is it possible to regard Christianity as the absolute religion or 'the changeless, exhaustive, and unconditioned realization of that which is conceived as the universal principle of religion'.[58] To regard it as the most perfect expression of the essence of religion is untenable.[59] In Troeltsch's view, Christianity is above all a particular, historical religion determined to a great extent by the different circumstances of life. It assumes different forms depending on the intellectual and social conditions in which it finds itself; it is culturally determined.

Gandhi would approve of Troeltsch's insistence that religious groups belonging to different cultures experience manifestations of the Divine Life that are as valid for them as the Christian manifestation of the Divine Life is for Christians. He would also applaud Troeltsch's view that the primary concern should be for mutual understanding between religions rather than conversion from one religion to another. Both would agree that all religions have a common goal in the Beyond, and a common ground in the Divine Spirit, but for Troeltsch historical religions manifest individual differences that are likely to remain:

so far as the eye can penetrate into the future, it would seem probable that the great revelations to the various civilizations will remain distinct ... and that the question of their several relative values will never be capable of objective determination, since every proof thereof will presuppose the special characteristics of the civilization in which it arises.[60]

Both would insist that mutual understanding occurs when each religion seeks to realize its own potential, yet at the same time is open to the influences of others in their quest for truth. Both would agree also that the 'earthly experience of the Divine Life is not One but Many'.[61]

As we have seen the type of religious education that Gandhi favours for schools is that which is open to the study of religions other than one's own. He supports the introduction of an open-ended approach to the teaching of religion, and is favourably disposed to what we would refer to today as religious pluralism. He commends the attempt to understand and appreciate the different beliefs and doctrines of the great religions of the world on the grounds that it can lead to a better appreciation of one's own faith.[62] Hence he would not approve of the narrow, exclusive, dogmatic approach to religious education. For this reason he would reject the exclusive attitude of theologians like Karl Barth for whom religion is unbelief, and revelation confined to the Word contained in Scripture, proclaimed in the Church, and incarnate in Christ. For Barth religion is at best an indication of man's perverted response to God's initiative and at worse a manifestation of man's revolt against God. The Church alone is the locus of faith, and of religion in the true sense of the term. This is the case not because of a process of differentiation conducted on the basis of an analysis of the general concept of religion, but as a consequence of God's self-revelation through his grace. Religion, as generally understood, is man's substitute for revelation. It cannot provide knowledge of God because there is no continuity between religion and revelation; the one radically displaces the other. Only when religion is sanctified by revelation can it be considered to be true.[63]

It follows that, in Barth's view, the Christian religion, as much as the non-Christian religions, stands under the judgement of unbelief pronounced on all manifestations of religion. The Church must never forsake its belief in the sufficiency of God's grace nor must it seek to resist other religions by appealing to religious experience or religious self-consciousness. Its truth lies not in its inherent holiness or its religious experience—an implicit criticism of Schleiermacher— but in the knowledge of God's grace and revelation through faith.[64]

The uniqueness of Scriptural revelation is further emphasized by Barth when he speaks of the biblical meaning of revelation as the self-unveiling of God who by his nature is inscrutable to man. The *Deus revelatus* is the *Deus absconditus*, 'the God to whom there is no way and no bridge, of whom we could not say or have to say one single word, has He not of His own initiative met us as *Deus revelatus*'.[65] He unveils himself to man who has no power to unveil him and the form he takes is the *humanitas Christi*. But it is not the form that reveals, but God in the form.[66] God the Father is God the Creator; God the Son is God as Reconciler; and God the Holy Spirit is God as Redeemer.[67] It is this Trinitarian doctrine which, according to Barth, 'marks off the Christian concept of revelation as Christian, in face of all other concepts of God and concepts of revelation'.[68] When we ask the question who God is, the Bible answers in such a way as to point us to the three-in-oneness of God.[69]

Needless to say this exclusivist attitude is contrary to the more open-ended approach to religious education favoured by Gandhi, and he would be equally opposed to the more modified form of exclusivism put forward by Emil Brunner, for whom Christian revelation is absolute, and different in kind from the revelation to be found in other religions despite apparent similarities. The history of religions, according to Brunner, cannot point to a religious system that is fully spiritual, consisting of personal, revealed, and ethical elements, or a religion in which the truly human and truly divine are one. That can be found 'only in that which is more than religion, in the divine revelation in Jesus Christ'.[70]

Gandhi acknowledges only too readily, however, that he had not been able to convince many people of the correctness of his views on education,[71] and that would apply to his views on both religious and secular education. The fact that he failed to convince people, however, does not mean that his views were insignificant. In many ways they were too avant garde for his time, which may have been one of the reasons why they were not always acceptable to his contemporaries.

Notes

1. *The Collected Works of Mahatma Gandhi* (hereafter, CWMG), Second Revised Edition, Ministry of Information and Broadcasting, Government of India, New Delhi, 1969–, Vol. 7, p. 428
2. CWMG, Vol. 8, p. 171
3. A.N. Whitehead, *An Anthology*, selected by F.S.C. Northrop & Mason W. Gross, Cambridge University Press, Cambridge, 1953, p. 100
4. CWMG, Vol. 22, p. 229
5. Ibid., Vol. 47, p. 422
6. Ibid., Vol. 56, p. 70
7. Ibid., p. 295

8. CWMG, Vol. 26, p. 117
9. Ibid., Vol. 25, p. 584; Vol. 30, p. 58
10. Ibid., Vol. 26, pp. 275–6
11. Ibid., Vol. 34, p. 515; Vol. 16, p. 362
12. Ibid., Vol. 50, p. 182; Vol. 58, p. 183
13. Ibid., Vol. 9, p. 196
14. Ibid., p. 475
15. Ibid., Vol. 56, p. 290; Vol. 63, p. 396; Vol. 30, p. 58
16. Ibid., Vol. 65, pp. 74, 450; Vol. 73, p. 235
17. Ibid., Vol 30, pp. 58–9
18. Ibid., Vol. 53, p. 366
19. Ibid., Vol. 42, p. 89
20. Ibid., Vol. 62, p. 436
21. M.K. Gandhi, *All Men are Brothers*, edited by Krishna Kripalani, UNESCO, Paris, 1958, 1969, p. 59
22. *The Complete Works of Vivekananda*, Vol. I, Advaita Ashrama, Calcutta, 1970, p. 356
23. Ibid., Vol. II, p. 133
24. Ibid., Vol. II, pp. 254, 334, 381
25. Ibid., Vol. I, p. 17
26. Ibid., Vol. II, p. 253
27. Ibid., Vol. I, p. 373
28. Ibid., Vol. I, pp. 374–5
29. Ibid., Vol. I, pp. 325, 365
30. Ibid., Vol. II, pp. 153, 235–6
31. Ibid., Vol. I, pp. 389–90
32. Ibid., Vol. I, pp. 317–8, 324
33. Ibid., Vol. II, p. 388
34. *All Men are Brothers*, pp. 54, 56, 59; N.K. Bose, *Selections from Gandhi*, Navajivan Trust, Ahmedabad, 1948, 1972, pp. 245–7
35. CWMG, Vol. 34, p. 515; Vol. 16, p. 362
36. Ibid., Vol. 50, p. 182; Vol. 58, p. 183
37. Ibid., Vol. 9, p. 139
38. Ibid., Vol. 37, pp. 254–5; cf. *The Selected Works of Mahatma Gandhi*, Navajivan Trust, Ahmedabad, Vol. VI, p. 519
39. *Selections from Gandhi*, p. 298
40. CWMG, Vol 49, pp. 241–2
41. Ibid., Vol. 34, pp. 394
42. Ibid., Vol. 37, pp. 254–5
43. Ibid., p. 255
44. Ninian Smart, *Secular Education and the Logic of Religion*, Heslington Lectures, University of York, 1966, Faber and Faber, London, 1968, p. 94
45. Ibid., p. 90

46. Ibid., p. 91
47. Ibid., p. 97
48. Ibid., p. 98
49. John Hick, *God and the Universe of Faiths*, Collins, Glasgow, 1977, pp. 138–9
50. John Hick, *God Has Many Names*, Macmillan, London, 1980, pp. 8, 58, 61, 81
51. John Hick, 'Jesus and the World Religions', *The Myth of God Incarnate*, edited by John Hick, SCM Press, London, 1977, p. 181
52. Raimundo Panikkar, *The Intra-Religious Dialogue*, Paulist Press, New York, 1978, p. 8
53. Ibid., pp. 26–30
54. Ibid., p. 31
55. Peter Winch, 'Understanding a Primitive Society', *Religion and Understanding*, edited by D.Z. Phillips, Blackwell, Oxford, 1967, p. 30
56. Ernst Troeltsch, 'The Place of Christianity Among the World Religions', in *Christian Thought: Its History and Application*, Meridian Books, New York, and University of London Press, London, 1957, pp. 35–63. Quoted from *Attitudes Towards Other Religions*, edited by Owen C. Thomas, Harper and Row, New York, 1969, p. 79
57. Ernst Troeltsch, *The Aboluteness of Christianity and the History of Religions*, S.C.M. Press, London, 1972, pp. 67–70
58. Ibid., p. 71
59. Ibid., p. 76
60. Ibid., p. 90
61. Ibid., p. 91
62. CWMG, Vol. 37, pp. 254–5; cf. *Selected Works*, Vol. VI, p. 519
63. Karl Barth, *Church Dogmatics*, Vol. I, Part 2, edited by G.W. Bromiley and T.F. Torrance, T. and T. Clark, Edinburgh, 1956, pp. 303f., 325f., 337f., 353f.,
64. Ibid., pp. 297–303, 307–310, 325–8, 332–3, 337–8, 353–4
65. Ibid., Vol.I, Part I, p. 368
66. Ibid., pp. 369, 371
67. Ibid., pp. 441f., 458f., 513f.
68. Ibid., p. 346
69. Ibid., p. 348
70. Emil Brunner, *Revelation and Reason*, translated by Olive Wyon, SCM Press, London, 1947, p. 270
71. CWMG, Vol. 54, p. 423

chapter six

Education and the Reformers

Gandhi's philosophy of education echoes the teachings of many of the reformers of Hinduism in modern India among whom was Rammohan Roy, who has been described as one of the most creative of nineteenth-century thinkers in India. What he sought above all to do in the field of education was to harmonize Western science and technology with the spirituality of the East for the benefit of mankind as a whole. His primary concern was that the native population of India might be provided with instruction in 'mathematics, natural philosophy, chemistry and anatomy and other useful sciences', rather than instruction in Sanskrit which the British sought to promote by means of the establishment of a new school in Calcutta.[1] Not that he was opposed to what he regards as the laudable desire of the government to improve the educational standards of the native population; but since the teaching of Sanskrit was already being undertaken in various parts of India under the able guidance of Hindu Pundits, remunerations and allowances to them would be a more effective way of promoting the study of the language than the establishment of a new school in Calcutta. Furthermore since Sanskrit was such a difficult language, requiring almost a lifetime of study to be truly mastered, a more liberal form of education embracing the natural sciences would improve the standard of education of the native population to a greater degree than the attempt to acquire mastery of Sanskrit. It is difficult not to conclude from the letter written by Roy to the Right Honourable William Pitt, Lord Amherst, that he regarded the time spent in acquiring what he calls 'the niceties of the Byakurun or Sangscrit Grammar'[2] as impractical, and that the establishment of a College in Calcutta, furnished with everything necessary for instruction in the sciences, would be a better use of government money, and more likely to achieve its aim to improve educational standards among the native population. This did not mean, however, that Roy was in any way averse to teaching the essentials of Hinduism; it was after all the way of life in which he had been nurtured. His *Vedānta grantha*, a Bengali translation of the Vedānta, which sought to establish the unity and supremacy of *Brahman* as Eternal Being, and his work on the Upanishads, in which he expounds the concept of *nirguṇa Brahman*, indicate that he was in the mainstream of Hindu thought. He defended it eloquently against those who would pour scorn on it, and ably rejected the objections of Christian missionaries of Serampore contained in their weekly newspaper *Samachar Darpan*. What his emphasis on rationality points to is a deep-seated desire on his part to restore the purity of Hinduism by the promotion of a lofty theism where no image or likeness of the Eternal, immutable *Brahman* would remain.[3] This is illustrated by the formation of the Brāhmo Samāj, a society he founded in 1828 to promote a lofty theism and to restore the religious purity of Hinduism. The society may have lacked popular appeal because of its intellectual bent, but it did succeed in creating an atmosphere of liberalism and rationality, and in providing a forum for reinterpreting the Hindu tradition. That his concern for rationality in the religious sphere should find similar expression in the field of education is not surprising. He was as ardent as Gandhi in his support for the use of the vernacular in teaching and learning and to this end he published a Bengali grammar of his own. His aim was to build a bridge between the old and new world through the promotion of mutual respect and understanding; the harmonization of Western science and technology with Eastern spirituality was simply a means to that end.

Gandhi, as we have seen, was deeply concerned with the need to use the vernacular rather than English as the medium of instruction in schools. In his view it was impractical, to say the least, to learn English before starting one's education when so much knowledge could be imparted equally effectively through the vernacular. Why should valuable time be wasted on acquiring competence in a foreign medium when native languages were just as effective? This approach echoes to a certain extent Roy's objections to the establishment of a new school for the study of Sanskrit in Calcutta. In the same way Roy's concern for the study of the sciences is reflected in the emphasis Gandhi places on the importance of handicrafts in education. But while Gandhi would support wholeheartedly Roy's endeavour to broaden the intellectual horizons of his fellow-countrymen, he would not have approved of a campaign against the teaching of Sanskrit which he considered to be the linguistic basis of Hindu culture.[4] Not that Roy engaged in such a campaign. His objection was limited to the establishment of a new school to teach Sanskrit when other opportunities existed in abundance.

Unlike Roy, Dayananda Sarasvati, one of the more influential figures in the history of modern India, was fully aware of the intimate connection between language, culture and national identity. He fully supported the teaching of Hindi and Sanskrit as national languages and advocated that both should be the medium of instruction in schools. He deplored the neglect of these languages to such an extent that he was reluctant to allow an English translation of his *Vedabhashya* to appear lest Sanskrit and Hindi should suffer as a consequence. As he says: 'the greatest drawback then is that the English-knowing people of India will on the appearance of the English translation of the *Vedabhashya* give up the Sanskrit and Hindi studies which they are so vehemently pursuing nowadays in order to enable themselves to read the *Vedabhashya*.'[5] Gandhi's reference to 'the tyranny of English', his belief that there could be 'no Swaraj without freedom from fondness of English',[6] and his awareness that real education was not possible for the people of India when the indigenous languages and culture of the nation were neglected, meant that he was in sympathy with the general thrust of the arguments put forward by Dayananda about the importance of language in relation to both self identity and national identity. Neither Gandhi nor Dayananda, however, was opposed to the teaching of English in schools. The latter recommended—despite the neglect of Sanskrit compared with the concern shown for the teaching of English, Urdu and Persian—that in a six-hour teaching day two hours should be devoted to teaching English, one hour to Urdu and Persian, and the remainder to the teaching of Sanskrit.[7] The former was of the opinion that 'every Hindu boy should learn Sanskrit'[8] Yet despite his insistence on the need for the use of the vernacular as the medium of instruction in schools, Gandhi sought to ensure at the same time that the windows of India were open to the winds of culture from other lands, since, in his view, the appreciation of the literary heritage of mankind could not be confined to the cultural heritage of India.

Gandhi's theory of education echoes also the teachings of Vivekananda. The latter recognized, like Roy, the significant contribution western science and technology could make to the material well-being of the people of India, but he was equally convinced that to progress spiritually it was necessary for western man to look to the east. The main tenet of his educational theory, however, is that learning should not be confined to the higher castes. He deplored the fact that most of the educational reforms of the preceding century had been to a greater or lesser degree ornamental and confined to the higher castes, who had been educated at the expense of the masses.[9] The main cause of India's parlous condition, in his view, was that education had been monopolized by a small number of people, and that if the country was to succeed in the future then education would have to be disseminated among the masses.[10] Radical reform in education was needed so that it could be made available to the lower classes, and not merely to the select few in the higher castes. The mass of ordinary people in India needed to be fully educated, and their eyes opened to the possibilities that existed in the world around them, in order 'to develop their lost individuality'.[11] The clear implication of this telling phrase is that without education the potential of the mass of people could not be realized, and they would fail to be truly human. Vivekananda is Kantian in his approach here for he sees that education has to do with our very identity as human beings and that without it we cease to be fully human. It was a demonstrable fact that little had been done for the masses in the past; they had been so down-trodden that they had forgotten they were human beings. But since universal education of the kind he advocated presented economic and methodological difficulties, Vivekananda suggests that the single-minded, self-sacrificing sannyasins should be organized to go from village to village to teach the masses in secular matters as well as religion, which they were already effectively teaching. Unfortunately, the poverty of India was such that boys would rather help their fathers in the fields, or make a living in some other way in order to help the family, than go to school. So Vivekananda suggests that 'if the mountain does not come to Mohammed, Mohammed must go to the mountain. If the poor boy cannot come to education, education must go to him'.[12]

The attempt by Vivekananda to improve the lot of ordinary people by providing them with similar educational opportunities open to the higher castes might be regarded as a form of *sarvodaya*. This philosophy determined Gandhi's approach to education, and, as we have shown, it was rooted in his belief in the essential unity of mankind and the indivisibility of Truth. For Gandhi, *sarvodaya* had to do especially with the status of women and the treatment of the untouchables in Hindu society, and it was primarily concerned with improving their standard of life. One of the ways in which their basic rights as human beings could be restored was by providing them with equality of opportunity in the field of education. His constructive programme, including his system of basic education, was directed to this end, and shows a clear similarity with the educational aims of Vivekananda.

In a speech on education delivered at Barsi in 1908 Tilak advocates the establishment of national schools in India, the curriculum of which should in the first instance provide for religious education since, in his view, secular studies were not enough in themselves to develop character. But he insists that it should be a tolerant form of religious education which would not be averse to the study of religions other than Hinduism. 'Secular education only is not enough to build up character. Religious education is necessary because the study of high principles keeps us away from evil pursuits.'[13] He maintains also that compulsory study of the English language should be abolished. This would avoid the necessity for students to spend twenty or more years mastering the language in order to obtain an education which could be easily acquired in seven or eight years through the medium of the vernacular.[14] In this respect his attitude to education is at one with that of Gandhi who, as we have seen, deplored the tyranny of English and was favourably disposed to a tolerant approach to religious education. He was firmly convinced that it was not possible to educate the people of India effectively through the medium of a foreign language and to the exclusion of the indigenous culture. An education of that sort cut people off from their roots and estranged them from their cultural heritage. He was aware also that the development of character demanded that religious education ought to form part of the school curriculum not religious education of a denominational kind, rather the study of the main tenets of all faiths since that promoted toleration and breadth of vision. It is significant that, like Tilak, Gandhi shows a remarkable openness to the study of world religions. He commends the teaching of ethics, for example, and the main tenets of other faiths because, as he says, understanding and appreciating the different beliefs and doctrines of the great religions of the world in a spirit of reverence and tolerance can only lead to a better appreciation of one's own faith.[15] Not for Gandhi, therefore, the narrow, exclusivist, dogmatic approach to religious education, or what he calls the religion of the prison house. He has no desire to confine religious education to instruction in the principles of the Hindu faith any more than he wishes the teaching of literature to be confined to the cultural heritage of India. In this respect he claims an affinity with Rammohan Roy as well as Tilak, and also, as we shall see, with Rabindranath Tagore, who wanted the windows of India to be opened wide to the winds of culture from other lands though not to the neglect of its own culture.[16] It is the inclusiveness of the phenomenological and historical approach to the study of religion rather than the exclusiveness of the traditional, dogmatic approach that appeals to Gandhi and the reformers, and in this respect they show commendable openness to religious studies and the acceptance of what is referred to today as religious pluralism.

Tilak and Gandhi were at one also in the way they linked education with *swarāj*. One of the primary objections raised by the British against granting home rule was that India was not fit for self-government because its people were deficient in education. Tilak's response to this objection was to cite the names of Akbar and Ashoka, and the empires of the Guptas and Rajputs, and to ask 'what ground was there to say that the descendants of those people who had governed those empires were today unfit to exercise that right? There was no disqualification, intellectual or physical which disabled them from taking part in the Government of any empire. They had shown their fitness in the past and were prepared to show it to-day if opportunities were granted to them.'[17] He expressed similar views earlier in a speech on Home Rule delivered at Belgaum on 1 May 1916, when he maintained that education would enable the people of India to learn how to manage their own affairs, and that 'the demand that the management of our affairs should be in our hands is the demand for *Swarajya*'.[18]

For Gandhi also education and *swarāj* went hand in hand, and an illustration of this is the way he claimed that the resources for education in schools could be derived from the sale of handicrafts. His advocacy of the spinning-wheel, as we have shown, was as much symbolic as practical, for while handicrafts provided resources for the educational programme he envisaged, they pointed at the same time to the importance of self-reliance as the starting point of the quest for self-rule and *swarāj*. It is clearly possible to see a link between the significance he attaches to self-belief and self-reliance, which the spinning-wheel epitomizes, and which the place of handicrafts in the school curriculum signifies, and his support for the use of home-spun cloth, or *khādī*, and his advocacy of *swadeshī* and *swarāj*. In a speech delivered at a municipal reception at Berhampur on March 29, 1921, for instance, he insists that support for national education under *swarāj* could come from the spinning-wheel, that the aim of education should be self-reliance, and that handicrafts should be as much an essential part of the educational programme as Hindi.[19] This view is echoed in his speech at a teacher's training camp at Brindaban on 4 May 1939, when he claims that a man could not be considered intelligent if his intellect was not correlated with his hands.[20] During a discussion with trainee teachers in the same year, as we have shown, he was asked whether handicrafts would not give way in due course to industrialization, and whether basic education of this sort really met the needs of India. His reply was that there would always be villages in India, and that the education of the country had to be revolutionized in order that the brain might be educated through the hand, and that we might be taught to discriminate between good and bad, right and wrong. In the past, he claims, the prevailing view had been to add handicrafts to the existing curriculum but this was a mistaken idea. It was necessary for the well-being of the people of India that the educational programme correlate crafts with the intellectual quest for knowledge.[21] Clearly Gandhi did not favour the view that handicrafts be considered an afterthought in the school curriculum. They were essential to the educational programme not only because of the resources they provided, but also because they promoted self-belief and self-reliance which were the essential prerequisites of *swarāj*.

Gokhale, like Tilak, was a Maharashtrian, and shared with him a love of the cultural heritage and traditions of the Marathi-speaking people, but he differed in temperament from Tilak in many ways. He believed, for example, that the only way to emancipate women from their bondage to a demeaning way of life was to ensure that they were provided with educational opportunities. Tilak maintained that a woman's place was in the home. In this respect Gandhi, who favoured the education of women in order that their lot in society might be improved, was closer to Gokhale than to Tilak. His kinship with

Gokhale is further evident in the similarity of their attitudes to elementary education. Gokhale sought to introduce a bill in the Imperial Legislative Council requesting permission to make better provision for the extension of elementary education in India on the grounds that it was of prime importance to remove illiteracy from society. But, in his view, provision of elementary education for the masses implied more than just removing illiteracy: it meant producing ultimately a higher level of intelligence in the community generally, a more refined standard of living, a keener enjoyment of life, and greater moral and economic efficiency for the individual. He goes on:

He who reckons these advantages lightly may as well doubt the value of light or fresh air in the economy of human health. I think it not unfair to say that one important test of the solicitude of a Government for the true well being of its people is the extent to which, and the manner in which, it seeks to discharge its duty in the matter of mass education. And judged by this test, the Government of this country must wake up to its responsibilities much more than it has hitherto done, before it can take its proper place among the civilised Governments of the world.[22]

Gandhi's plan for primary education certainly involved a greater degree of literacy among the masses and it is significant that he sent a letter to Gokhale on 13 January 1905 requesting his assistance in providing graduates from his College in Poona, namely, Fergusson College, to teach in a boarding school he proposed to open for Indian children.[23] But Gandhi also believed that the teaching of handicrafts could act as the spearhead of a silent revolution in education, and go a long way towards eliminating some of the worst evils of society by laying the foundation of a more just and equitable social order.[24]

Gokhale and Gandhi are agreed in their approach to the education of women. The former refers to the bondage of caste and custom that had kept many tied down to fixed ways of life and forms of thought and had prevented all efforts to introduce even the most elementary reforms. This was particularly true in the case of women who, because they were denied access to any form of intellectual pursuit, and suffered from enforced ignorance, were willing victims of unjust and harmful customs. Because of this Gokhale argues:

It is obvious that, under the circumstances, a wide diffusion of education, with all its solvent influences, among the women of India, is the only means of emancipating their minds from this degrading thraldom to ideas inherited through a long past and that such emancipation will not only restore women to the honoured position which they at one time occupied in India, but will also facilitate, more than anything else, our assimilation of those elements of Western civilization without which all thoughts of India's regeneration are mere idle dreams, and all attempts at it foredoomed to failure.[25]

So Gokhale, unlike Roy, sees social amelioration, and improvement in the lot of women as a prerequisite of the harmonization of Western science and Eastern spirituality. For Gandhi, as we have seen, the policy of *sarvodaya* concerned the status of women and the treatment of the untouchables in Hindu society, and was primarily directed at improving their standard of life. His view is that one of the ways in which their basic rights as human beings could be established was by providing them with equality of opportunity in the field of education, and his constructive programme, with its emphasis on basic education, was directed to that end.

Rabindranath Tagore's pursuit of his religious, cultural and educational ideals led him to establish the Vishva Bharati University at Shantiniketan, where, in a residential setting in close proximity with nature, he sought to show that the purpose of education was the emancipation of the soul and the liberation of the human spirit. In pursuit of this goal, which might be regarded as essentially Platonic, he recognized that it was not enough to impart information, or develop the mind or intellect alone. It was necessary rather to cultivate the whole man, body, mind and spirit, and to achieve this end it was important to pay particular attention to the atmosphere and environment in which education was imparted, and to the languages that were to be used in the process. The rural nature of the setting of the university reflects Tagore's views on the relation between God, man and nature. 'If we had to build a school that would serve as a model, we should see that it was situated in a quiet spot far from the crowded city, and had the natural advantages of open sky, fields, trees, and the like. It should be a retreat where teachers and students would live dedicated to learning.'[26] The same power that created the universe, he maintains, enlightens man's consciousness, and the ultimate goal is to attain to the perfection of the Absolute through the realization of the divine in the soul.'In the history of man moments have come when we have heard the music of God's life touching man's life in perfect harmony. We have known the fulfilment of man's personality in gaining God's nature for itself, in utter self-giving out of abundance of love.'[27] This is in line with Gandhi's teaching that no distinction can be drawn between the *Ātman* within, and God or Truth, and with the teaching of *Advaita Vedānta* concerning the *Ātman-Brahman* identity. It reflects also his belief that the primary aim of education, or true education as he calls it, is self-knowledge and the cultivation of the qualities of courage, virtue and self-denial.[28]

Tagore's emphasis on the importance of the mother tongue as the means of instruction in education, and on the need for the harmonious development of all man's faculties, not just the mind in isolation from the body and spirit, bears a close resemblance to the ideals of Gandhi, whose educational concerns are rooted in his fundamental belief about the true nature of the Self. The system of education introduced by the British did not contribute to the moral and spiritual well-being of the people of India. In Gandhi's view it served rather to separate pupils from their parents, and alienate them from their cultural heritage, thereby undermining their knowledge of themselves, and creating problems of self-identity. In a letter written to Tagore on 21 January 1918, he enquired whether teaching in the schools and colleges of India should not be effected through the vernacular, and whether Hindi should not be made 'a compulsory second language in all post-primary schools'.[29] Tagore acknowledged that mastering the English language in itself was difficult enough, but acquiring an understanding of English thought, and absorbing English ideas in order to use them in everyday life, was even more difficult. It was not possible, in his view, for education and life to become one in such circumstances: that was only possible through the use of the vernacular.[30] Furthermore, since schools should be at the heart of society, and in constant touch with economic, intellectual, aesthetic, social and spiritual affairs, that goal was only possible when education and life were integrated.[31] Even so, Tagore, like Gandhi, had no antipathy to, or distrust of, other cultures because of their alien character. He believed that there should be no obstacles to cultural exchange between east and west, and that western ideas should be welcomed rather than resisted, so that in due course they might be assimilated into the Hindu way of life, and become a source of strength and nourishment to the culture of the nation. 'I deeply hope that our educational centres will be the meeting ground of the East and the West. In the world of material gain human beings have neither stopped fighting, nor will they easily do so. But there are no obstacles to their meeting in the field of cultural exchange.'[32]

Gandhi's theory of education is reflected also in the teachings of his ardent disciple Vinoba Bhave, who learned much from him at the Sabarmati ashram near Ahmedabad. It was Bhave's contention that with the establishment of *lok-niti*,—government of the people,—and by the people,—and with the development of *gramraj*, village government, went the responsibility of educating people to a sufficient degree of competence that they were able to manage their own affairs. His concept of *Nai Talim*, new education, or education for life, meant establishing a *vidyapith*, a seat of learning, or university, in every village, in order to provide a complete education for those who desired it.[33] For Bhave, this meant education for life, which meant that no hard-and-fast distinction could be drawn between work and learning: they were to be regarded as two sides of the same coin. The old form of education distinguished between mental and manual labour. *Nai Talim*, on the other hand, gave equal value to both, and integrated them to form a comprehensive whole.[34] Here Bhave is supporting Gandhi's emphasis on combining the hand and brain, or handicrafts and literacy, in the educational programme. But he carries it forward further by insisting on the fundamental unity of mental and bodily activities. He is at one with Gandhi also, when he refers to the teaching of religion as not simply a literary or cultural matter, but as something which is concerned with the cultivation of a sound character.'My own point of view is that true religious teaching is not a matter of literature. The essence of religion is a sound character, faith in God, and the conviction that the soul is other than the body.'[35] Again his stress on the importance of self-knowledge in the educational process, echoes much of what Gandhi has to say about true education, and the significance of the *Ātman-Brahman* identity. 'The most important thing for any kind of education, whether in school or in society, is to bring about the recognition that we are other than our bodies. It is this self-knowledge which is the foundation on which the power of *satyāgraha* can be built.'[36] Bhave is generally considered to be a most worthy disciple of Gandhi and this applies particularly to his thoughts on education.

Radhakrishnan's emphasis on what he calls the religion of the spirit, and his philosophical approach to the interpretation of the Hindu way of life, does not mean that he had little to say on the question of the importance of education in the development of modern India. His social philosophy is concerned with both politics and education, and on the question of the latter he makes the point that there is little to be said in favour of that type of education which stimulates the mind without satisfying it.[37] He recognizes, however, that much effort, or 'alchemy of spirit' as he calls it, is required to fuse different fields of knowledge and diverse specializations into a coherent whole, or a comprehensive body of wisdom.[38] This leads him to conclude that wisdom is not easily come by, and that intellectual opinions are no substitute for spiritual experience.[39] His mature judgment is that the main purpose of education is self-knowledge[40] and that the ultimate goal is the unification of the outer and inner man[41]. No form of education will succeed, in his view, which does not teach us to live well.[42] So higher education, while being mindful of contemporary events, should aim to inculcate an outlook on life that will revere eternal values, and preserve the integrity of man's soul.[43]

This emphasis on self-knowledge and the importance of a moral way of life, reflects what Gandhi has to say about the isomorphism of *Satya* and *Sat*, and what the Upanishads refer to as the identity of *Ātman-Brahman*. The goal of education for Gandhi, as for Radhakrishnan, is to know the Self, and true education is the recognition that no distinction can be drawn between the *Ātman* and *Satya*, the Self and Truth, or the soul and God.

From what has been said here, albeit briefly, it can be deduced that Gandhi's thoughts on education echo much of what earlier reformers had to say on the subject, and that so far as his approach to education is concerned, he upheld the traditions of the Hindu reformers, and exercised a significant influence on those who came after him.

Notes

1. *English Works of Raja Rammohun Roy*, edited by Dr Kalidas Nag and Debajyoti Burman, Sadaran Brahmo Samaj, Calcutta, 1945-51, Part IV, 1946, pp. 105–8
2. Ibid.
3. Ibid., pp. 59–116, passim
4. *M.K. Gandhi: An Autobiography*, Jonathan Cape, London 1972, pp. 15,16
5. *Autobiography of Dayananda Sarasvati*, edited by K.C. Yadav, Second Revised Edition, Manohar Publications, New Delhi, 1978, p. 65

6. *The Collected Works of Mahatma Gandhi* (hereafter, CWMG), Vol. 13, p. 359

7. *Autobiography of Dayananda Sarasvati*, 70

8. CWMG, Vol. 13, 358

9. *The Complete Works of Swami Vivekananda*, Vols. I-VIII, Advaita Ashram, Calcutta, 1970, Vol III, p. 216

10. Ibid., Vol. IV, p. 481

11. Ibid., Vol. IV, pp. 362–3

12. Ibid.

13. *Bal Gangadhar Tilak: His Writings and Speeches*, Third Edition, Ganesh and Co., Madras, 1922, p. 83

14. Ibid., pp. 83–6

15. *The Selected Works of Mahatma Gandhi*, Navajivan Trust, Ahmedabad, 1968, Vol. VI, p. 519

16. N.K. Bose, *Selections from Gandhi*, Navajivan Trust, Ahmedabad, 1948, 1972, p. 298

17. *Tilak: His Writings and Speeches*, pp. 254–5

18. Ibid., pp. 117–8

19. CWMG, Vol. 19, p. 484

20. Ibid., Vol. 69, p. 205

21. Ibid., pp. 370–77

22. *Speeches of Gopal Krishna Gokhale*, Third Edition, G.A. Natesan and Co., Madras, 1920, p. 608

23. CWMG, Vol. 4, pp. 332–3

24. *Selected Works*, VI, pp. 507, 512

25. *Speeches of Gopal Krishna Gokhale*, pp. 882–3

26. Rabindranath Tagore, *Towards Universal Man*, Asia Publishing House, Bombay, 1961, p. 75.

27. Rabindranath Tagore, *Personality: Lectures Delivered in America*, Macmillan, London, 1921, p. 106.

28. *Selections from Gandhi*, p. 288

29. CWMG, Vol. 14, p. 163

30. *Towards Universal Man*, pp. 43–46

31. Ibid., pp. 202–3.

32. Ibid., p. 250

33. Vinoba Bhave, *Democratic Values and the Practice of Citizenship, Selections from the Addresses of Vinoba Bhāve 1951–1968*, translated by Marjorie Sykes, Sarva Seva Sangh Prakashan, Kashi, Rajghat, Varanasi, 1962, p. 99

34. Vinoba Bhave, *Thoughts on Education*, Akhil Bharat Sarva Seva Sangh, Rajghat, Kashi, Varanasi, 1959, p. 234

35. Ibid., p. 117

36. Ibid., p. 252

37. Sarvepalli Radhakrishnan, *Kalki or the Future of Civilisation*, Kegan and Paul, London 1929, p. 36. Cf. George P. Conger, 'Radhakrishnan's World', *The Philosophy of Sarvepalli Radhakrishnan*, edited by Paul Arthur Schilpp, Motilal Banarsidass, Delhi, 1992, p. 98
38. Sarvepalli Radhakrishnan, *Education, Politics and War*, International Book Service, Poona, 1944, p. 105. Cf. Conger, *op. cit.* p. 98
39. Ibid., p. 106
40. Ibid., p. 101
41. Ibid., p. 106
42. Ibid., pp. 28 and 88
43. Ibid., p. 175

chapter seven

Theories of Education

In some respects Gandhi's attitude to education is reminiscent of Plato's. For the latter, education is the best thing that a person could ever have,[1] and the importance he attaches to it is evidenced by the fact that he did not believe children should be brought into the world unless their parents were always prepared to nurture them and provide them with an education.[2] The type of education Plato favours is one directed towards the cultivation of the soul as the ultimate goal, and to this end he regards gymnastics and music as necessary prerequisites. The question he poses in the *Crito*, to which Socrates replies in the affirmative, bears this out: 'Were not the laws which have the charge of education right in commanding your father to train you in music and gymnastic?'[3] This favoured form of education is outlined in the *Protagoras*, where it is proposed that pupils be taught the use of the lyre, and introduced to the works of the poets, 'in order that they may learn to be more gentle and harmonious, and rhythmical, and so more fitted for speech and action'. Following this it is proposed that they should be entrusted to the master of gymnastics so that their bodies may better serve their minds.[4] Yet, as Rousseau maintains, it is *The Republic* which must be regarded as 'the finest treatise on Education ever written', because it provides us with an account of what Plato considered to be the best form of public education.[5]

The Republic is ostensibly an enquiry into the nature of justice, but since justice is a social virtue, Plato finds it necessary to examine the way in which it would be administered in an ideal state where industrial, military and ruling classes prevail. These social divisions within the ideal state, according to Plato, correspond to distinctions created by God within the soul. They find mythical expression in *The Republic* as bronze, silver and gold: 'God as he was fashioning you, put gold in those of you who are capable of ruling...silver in the auxiliaries, and iron and copper in the farmers and other craftsmen.'[6] The administration of justice within the ideal state, however, would necessarily depend on the proper education and training of the respective classes referred to. But while great attention is paid to the education of the rulers or guardians, and soldiers or auxiliaries, little mention is made of the education of the industrial or bronze class. Presumably for Plato, with his aristocratic bent, some form of vocational training would be considered to be sufficient for this class since intellectual and moral excellence could be achieved only by the guardians.[7] It is evident that the education of the gold and silver classes had intellectual integrity and high standards of morality as its goal. But Plato's theory of education is concerned also with the welfare and happiness of all classes, or *sarvodaya* as Gandhi would call it, and this form of education, as we have noted, involved training in music and gymnastics, both designed ultimately for the cultivation of the soul.[8]

It should be noted, however, that music for Plato is not confined to what the term normally implies, but includes literature involving narratives of both the allegorical and literary kind. Yet not all kinds of tales should be taught to the young: only those that could be relied upon to promote virtuous thoughts. For example, the narrative of Hephaestus binding Hera his mother, and being thrown from heaven by his father: 'when his mother was being beaten and he tried to defend her, and all the tales of the battles of the giants that Homer has made, these stories we shall not receive into our city, whether they purport to be allegorical or not'.[9] This arbitrary censorship of narratives would not have endeared Plato to the more liberally minded of critics perhaps, but the principle he seems to have adopted is that some tales are good and others bad, and that only those tales which honour the gods are to be told if we consider the promotion of virtue to be the ultimate goal.[10] What applies to the gods applies equally to stories about heroes and departed souls; all reference to the weeping and wailing of famous men, and derogatory remarks about the other world, should be removed from tales taught to children.[11] Great importance also should be attached to the pursuit of truth and the exercise of self-control, and stories of heroes should incorporate these virtues. Yet, according to Plato, only rulers should be permitted to lie or, as it is currently expressed, be economical with the truth, and even then only in pursuance of the public good.[12]

Music in its traditional sense for Plato is required to include harmonies that promote courage, and rhythms that are in accord with the moral disposition of the soul. What this means is that all effeminate and convivial musical forms, (and it would be interesting to speculate what their modern equivalents might be), should be discarded. For Plato then, musical training is considered to be extremely potent, because in his view 'rhythm and harmony enter most powerfully into the innermost part of the soul...bearing grace with them, so making graceful him who is rightly trained, and him who is not, the reverse.'[13] The same applies to other forms of arts and crafts: only those forms of art that promote virtue are to be tolerated. 'We must seek out those craftsmen who have the happy gift of tracing out the nature of the fair and graceful, that our young men may dwell as in a health-giving region where all that surrounds them is beneficent.' It follows that they must be allowed to experience fair works of art, which will be like a health-giving breeze from a purer region, and which will lead them from their earliest years 'into likeness and friendship and harmony with the principle of beauty'.[14] This sentiment is echoed by Aristotle when he maintains that all that is mean and low should be banished from the sight of the young.[15]

In contrast to his fairly comprehensive treatment of music however, what Plato has to say about gymnastics is circumscribed and limited. Nevertheless, he does maintain that there is a mutual interaction between body and soul, and that they tend to influence each other. That being the case, gymnastics like music should be introduced at an early age into the educational process and continue throughout life. But certain forms of self-control should be encouraged, and excessive preoccupation with gymnastics deplored, on the grounds that it can lead to uncivilized behaviour and make a man 'devoid of all rhythm and grace'.[16] So the main aim of gymnastics for Plato, is the preservation of dignity and freedom and the promotion of health, agility, beauty, and harmonious motion.[17] And the purpose of both music and gymnastics is to harmonize the two elements of the soul, namely, the 'spirited' and the 'philosophic'.[18]

Higher education on the other hand, in contrast to what Gandhi has to say on the subject, is reserved for the guardians or rulers and philosophers; for those who display the qualities of nobility, graciousness and generosity. They would necessarily possess such natural gifts as 'courage, loftiness of spirit, readiness of learning, and memory' and be 'ready learners, lofty-minded, and gracious, lovers and kinsmen of truth, justice, courage, and temperance'.[19] The ultimate aim of higher education, for Plato, is not the accumulation of knowledge, but the conversion of the soul from study of the sensible world, 'from a day as dark as night', to contemplation of real existence, 'to the true ascent which leads towards being'.[20] So his view is that the education of the guardians of the state should be characterized by contemplation of the transcendental rather than the empirical sphere of existence; the realm of being rather than the realm of becoming. His argument is that educators were misguided when they maintained they could impart knowledge to the soul which it did not possess already, or which was not already there. He argues:

the power and capacity of learning exist in the soul already; and that just as the eye is unable to turn from darkness to light without the whole body, so too the instrument of knowledge can only by the movement of the whole soul be turned from the world of becoming into that of being, and learn by degrees to endure the sight of being, and of the brightest and best of being, or in other words, of the good.[21]

Plato's scheme of higher education involves progression from arithmetic, geometry and astronomy to dialectics, or from mathematics to metaphysics, as it is sometimes described. By stressing the importance of training in abstract thought, which both these disciplines favoured, especially mathematics, he was displaying Pythagorean influences, and his awareness of the philosophy that considered number to be the essence of all things. His desire to include geometry in the higher educational curriculum points to his belief that it is a discipline that 'will draw the soul towards the truth, and create the spirit of philosophy'.[22] Hence his insistence that guardians of the ideal state should be well versed in the intricacies of the subject, and also in the essentials of astronomy, the pursuit of which, in his view, purifies and illuminates the eye of the soul enabling truth to be perceived.[23]

Yet absolute truth, in Plato's view, is revealed only by means of dialectics, the highest discipline, which proceeds, it is true, with the help of the sciences, but without their assumptions or presuppositions. He reminds us that 'the power of dialectic alone' reveals absolute truth, and then only to those who were previously disciples of the sciences. Only the dialectic method operates from first principles, and dialectics is the only science which does away with hypotheses in order to secure its ground. 'The eye of the soul embedded in what is really a swamp of barbarism', is by the gentle aid of dialectics raised upwards, 'using the arts we have enumerated as handmaids in the work of conversion'.[24] So would-be rulers of the ideal state need to attend to philosophical studies, or dialectics, the bed-rock of the sciences, if they would fulfil their task successfully.[25]

That Plato should regard his educational scheme as one designed for women as well as men is significant in the light of the comparisons being drawn with Gandhi's philosophy of education.[26] His considered view is that while women may be physically weaker than men, it does not follow that they are not equally capable of governing or acting as rulers or guardians of the state. So education, for him, should be open to both sexes and directed towards the cultivation of virtue; it is that which makes both men and women pursue the ideal of perfection, and it is the only kind of education which is worthy of the name. Other forms of education and 'that other sort of training, which aims at the acquisition of wealth or bodily strength, or mere cleverness apart from intelligence and justice, is mean and illiberal, and is not worthy to be called education at all'.[27]

In contrast to Gandhi, Plato had little to say about the education of artisans apart from stating that if they were particularly good at anything they should practise it. The good husbandman, for example, should practise tilling the ground; the carpenter should learn to measure correctly; the teacher should direct the child's inclinations; and the builder should practice building houses.[28] Yet despite this omission in Plato's theory of education, there is ample justification for Whitehead's oft-quoted view that the European philosophical tradition, 'consists of a series of footnotes to Plato' and that the Platonic ideal has been of inestimable value to European civilization by promoting the spirit of curiosity which is at the heart of scientific investigation; by encouraging the arts; and by insisting on the importance of human dignity and the pursuit of virtue.[29] It is appropriate to note at this point that dignity and virtue were paramount among Gandhi's ideals, and to the forefront of his philosophy of education. Like Plato too, he favoured the education of both sexes, as his emphasis on the importance of *sarvodaya* exemplifies, but with the significant difference that he supported the concept of higher education for all and not just the few. Similarities between them on the ultimate purpose of education is also worthy of note. Plato sees the ultimate aim of higher education as the conversion of the soul from study of the sensible world to contemplation of real existence, and not the accumulation of knowledge. True education for Gandhi also is the nurture of the soul, the Ātman; the promotion of self-knowledge and self-fulfilment; the development of character; and the cultivation of the whole man, body, mind, and spirit. Ultimately this was the only kind of education, in his view, that would produce the uplift of society as a whole.

There is a case to be made also for drawing a comparison between Gandhi's theory of education and that of Tillich. In an address on the theology of education, the latter refers to three main educational aims, namely, technical, humanistic, and inductive.[30] Technical education, as the term implies, is, for him, the type of education that would enable us to exercise skills in the field of arts and crafts. During the middle ages up to the Reformation it was combined with the inductive type of education, which promotes the participation of the individual in the life of the group. Modern liberal education, on the other hand, combines elements of the technical with that of the humanistic type of education, which seeks the realization of human potential. The more revolutionary twentieth-century movements combine technical and inductive educational elements after the medieval fashion.

The humanistic form of education has, for Tillich, many different elements including intellectual discipline, knowledge of the subject matter, and concern for a proper relationship between individual pursuits and the community as a whole. But its main aim is the realization of the individual and social potential of all human beings. He acknowledges that this is the legacy of the Renaissance, and the philosophy that has dominated our thinking during recent centuries. Every individual, it is claimed, is unique and significant, and should be allowed to develop fully the talents he is endowed with, or, in other words, to actualize his potential freely.

The inductive form of education, on the other hand, finds its most significant expression in medieval culture. Its primary aim is not the development of individual potential as such but, through the use of institutions and symbols, to promote the participation of individuals in the life of the group. For example, it aims at promoting the induction of children into the life of the family, of citizens into the life of the nation, and of worshippers into the life of the church, the *corpus Christianum*. The spirit of medieval Christianity permeated education in the middle ages to such an extent that it imposed the inductive principle on every level of man's individual and social life, including his technical training in basic and specialist skills. 'The induction of the middle ages was induction into a community with symbols in which answers to the questions of human existence and its meaning were embodied. One can say that induction was initiation, initiation into the mystery of human existence.'[31] This inductive principle persisted and exercised great influence in those countries where the church continued to determine the spirit of education.

It is possible to maintain, as Gandhi shows, that the inductive principle was completely undermined in India by the introduction of a form of education that imposed an alien culture on the native population through the compulsory use of a foreign language as the medium of instruction. As Gandhi claims, this was a form of tyranny that divided members of the same family from one another, and those who participated in, or were subjected to, this form of education, were effectively separated from their roots in Indian society, and from their cultural heritage. In the process they were deprived of any sense of self-identity or national identity. Far from being inducted into the Indian community in which they were born, therefore, the educational system that prevailed in India at the time, served to induct them into an alien culture far removed from that in which they had been nurtured.

But possibly the same tragedy could have been experienced in India by the acceptance of a purely humanistic form of education. Stress on the uniqueness of the individual, or on the need to be allowed to develop or actualize one's potential, irrespective of the traditions or mores of the community in which one is nurtured, undermines to a similar extent one's sense of national identity, and effectively separates the individual from his roots in society. It can be argued that the need for roots is so strong that our lives as individuals are impoverished, and our self-identity undermined, when we are separated from our cultural heritage, and from participation in the way of life in which we were nurtured. We acquire an understanding of Truth, as Gandhi calls it, or an awareness of the mystery of human existence, to use Tillich's terminology, as participants in a way of life. If this is so, then there is a case to be made for the harmonization of the three aims of education enumerated by Tillich, namely, the technical, humanistic, and inductive.

In point of fact, Tillich examines further the correlation between the humanistic and inductive aims of education, and notes that while at first sight they appear to be conflicting aims, a resolution of the seeming differences is possible. He claims, for instance, that the humanistic spirit raises questions about the purpose of life, about the meaning of existence, and about life's ultimate goal. That is, it raises the questions: Who am I? Where am I going? What is the purpose of my life? These are radical questions about being itself; about personal existence and self-identity. They are existential questions which reflect the basic principles of humanism. Answers are anticipated, and this in itself points to a basic human need. The inductive form of education responds to this need, and through the use of symbols and institutions promotes the participation of individuals in the life of the group or society. Tillich, as we have seen, refers to inducting children into the life of the family, citizens into the life of the nation, and worshippers into the life of the church. So the inductive aim of education, when properly and successfully implemented, includes the principle of humanism. It correlates questions and answers, and allows for the free development of human potentialities within the life of the group. At the same time it incorporates all the aims of a technical education.

When we reflect on the consequences of the harmonization of the three aims of education Tillich refers to, it can be maintained that this is precisely what Gandhi's philosophy of education seeks to do. Technical education certainly has an important place in his proposed educational system, as his emphasis on the need for basic education indicates. Similarly he recognizes the importance of an inductive form of education which ensures that participants are not separated from their roots in society, or from their cultural heritage. His stress on the importance of the use of the vernacular as the means of instruction in schools is an indication of that fact. It can also be argued that the humanistic principle, which allows for the free development of the potential of the individual within the Indian way of life, is adequately provided for in his educational philosophy, as his programme of constructive, religious, and what he calls true education shows.

Gandhi's desire to combine the creativity of handicrafts with intellectual skills in the school curriculum is an indication that he strongly supported the Montessori method of teaching. When he first encountered Maria Montessori's educational programme he was favourably impressed by it and commended her for her innovative methods. He notes, for example, that under her guidance children learned as they played, and felt none of the strain sometimes associated with learning. They were encouraged to develop all their senses, and music and bodily exercises occupied a significant place in their programme. While little attention was paid to memorizing as such, much importance was attached to periods of concentration and silence.[32] Furthermore, she attached great importance to the environment in the learning process,[33] which appealed to Gandhi, and which also echoed Tagore's beliefs, which prompted him to establish the Visva Bharati University at Shantiniketan. There, in a residential setting in close proximity with nature, Tagore sought to show that the purpose of education was the emancipation of the soul, and the liberation of the human spirit. In pursuit of this goal, which might be regarded as essentially Platonic, he recognized that to educate a person it was not enough to impart information, or develop the mind and intellect alone; rather it was necessary to cultivate the whole person, body, mind, and spirit, and to achieve this end he considered the environment in which education was imparted to be of great importance. This approach is in line with Gandhi's teaching, when he refers to culture as the refinement of feelings; when he asserts that it is possible to imbibe culture as much from the environment as from the manner in which it is imparted; and when he claims that the primary aim of education is the cultivation of character.[34] In a letter to Manilal and Sushila Gandhi, dated 2 January 1935 he makes the point: 'Give up your fondness for schools. It is my firm belief that although the schools may offer you a free play for the intellect they do little towards character-building.'[35] So it is evident that he would approve of Montessori's stated aim: 'Give the child an environment in which everything is constituted in proportion to himself...Then there will develop within the child that "active life" which has caused so many to marvel because they see in it not only a simple exercise performed with pleasure but also the revelation of a spiritual life.'[36]

Given his desire to include vocational training and the teaching of handicrafts in his educational programme it is clear that Gandhi would be in agreement with Maria Montessori's conviction that the mental and physical powers of an individual should be inter-related; that 'mental development *must* be connected with movement and be dependent on it';[37] and that practical and didactic exercises, and sensory training, should all be used to liberate the child.[38] A similar agreement in their approach to educational methods might be discerned in what they have to say about crafts. For Montessori, education had to be understood as 'the active help given to the normal expansion of the life of the child'.[39] She discovered, for example, from her experience of teaching a mentally defective girl to weave and sew, that the latter was able to acquire greater control over her hand movements while sewing than she was able to do with other tasks. So, for her, the weaving of mats had a preparatory place in the educational programme.[40] Handicrafts, as we have seen, played an important part in Gandhi's educational programme also. He saw the need, as we have seen, to revolutionize the approach to education in order that the brain might be educated through the hand, and that we might thereby learn to discriminate between good and bad. The prevailing practice in education had been to add handicrafts to the existing curriculum. For Gandhi this was a mistaken view, since there were sound educational reasons for correlating crafts and intellectual knowledge.[41]

It is significant that Gandhi believed the teaching of handicrafts should be given pride of place in the education of children, and in propounding this view he was influenced, as we have noted, by two considerations. In the first place he had a high regard for the creative skills involved in producing artistic objects, and secondly, he believed that the sale of such objects produced by students might enable a school to become economically self-supporting.[42] Furthermore he was realistic enough to see that no compulsory system of education was likely to succeed unless it included some form of vocational training coupled with the economic self-sufficiency that could be derived from the sale of crafts produced by students. It was impossible, in his view, to exaggerate the harm done to the youth of the nation because of the belief that if they were educated it was not fitting for them to labour with their hands in order to earn their living.[43]

Montessori's view that the sense of touch was fundamental and primordial, and essential to the early years of a student's life if his future training was to be effective, was at one with Gandhi's belief that the education of the heart could be effected more by the touch of the teacher than through the medium of books. But this comment of Montessori on the primordial nature of the sense of touch, while referring specifically to the relationship that should exist between teacher and pupil, could in Gandhi's case be extended to apply to the importance he attached to vocational training and the craft of hand-spinning, which enabled student and teacher alike to keep in touch with the real world. Nothing was more demeaning and demoralizing, in his view, than that manual labour should be despised, since such an attitude reflected badly on the despiser himself and ultimately undermined the status of the nation.[44]

That Gandhi should approve so wholeheartedly of vocational training as an essential element in the national educational curriculum, is an indication that he was at one with the educational aims of A.N. Whitehead. The latter, despite his admiration for Plato's educational scheme, was critical of him for his lack of concern for technical education. Because of this, the negative aspect of Plato's programme was that the artisans fared badly in the ideal state compared with guardians and auxiliaries. Whitehead's belief is that education should be fully comprehensive, and that no curriculum could be regarded as complete without the inclusion of technical subjects.[45] On the other hand, he notes that the positive aspect of Plato's educational theory was the way it promoted art, encouraged the spirit of curiosity, which was the origin of science, and defended human dignity against those forces of materialism that tended to undermine it.[46] In this respect he is in agreement with Gandhi, for whom dignity and virtue were paramount, and as we have indicated, at the forefront of his educational philosophy as his emphasis on *sarvodaya* exemplifies.

Whitehead sees the primary purpose of education as concern for all aspects of life. In his view the only subject-matter for education is life in all its manifestations.[47] He sees no point in pumping inert knowledge into the minds of students.[48] True education has to be regarded as acquiring the art of utilizing knowledge, and learning how to apply theoretical ideas to practical issues. This ensures the vitality of knowledge and delivers it from inertia.[49] The acquisition of inert ideas was unfortunately characteristic of much education in the past, and nothing was more harmful and burdensome.[50] Pedants tended to sneer at the view that education should be useful, but, in Whitehead's view, if education is not useful, then it is of little value.[51] If there is lack of connection between subjects in the educational curriculum, then it tends to produce a loss of vitality. It leads to an inability on the part of students to see the wood for the trees, while the aim of education is to enable them to see the wood precisely because of the trees.[52] The methods that any satisfactory comprehensive system of education needs to employ, according to Whitehead, are three-fold, namely, literary, scientific, and technical. Students should be taught aesthetic appreciation, the spirit of scientific enquiry, and techniques for living.[53] The three methods are interrelated and should be harmonized in a comprehensive educational programme. A technical education in isolation from the literary and scientific aspects, he argues, would be far too narrow in its approach, and a literary or scientific education without the technical aspect would be unsatisfactory, and produce graduates ill-prepared for life in society.[54]

If Whitehead's concern for technical education puts him at odds with Plato, he speaks with the same voice as Gandhi. Like Gandhi, he favours an active rather than a passive approach to education, or active thought rather than 'inert ideas' as he calls it, and this is the reason why he is critical of contemporary education with its preoccupation with abstract theories rather than practical programmes. He refers to that approach as ideas being 'merely received into the mind without being utilised, or tested, or thrown into fresh combinations'.[55] He is dismissive of the type of education that consists simply in the passive reception of the ideas of others and deplores the antithesis drawn between a technical and a liberal education.[56] No technical education could be adequate without the liberal approach, and no liberal education could be deemed satisfactory without the technical approach.[57] His view is that a technical education 'emphasises manual skill, and the co-ordinated action of hand and eye',[58] but it requires also scientific knowledge and aesthetic appreciation, because there is 'a reciprocal influence between brain activity and material creative activity'.[59] One of the reasons for 'the brain-lethargy of aristocracies', he argues, is their failure to pursue the art of handcraft! So there is no alternative to a technical education, in his view, if we wish to 'obtain the full realization of truths as applying, and not as empty formulae', because it combines thinking and creative experience, that is, the 'experience which teaches you to co-ordinate act and thought, experience leading you to associate thought with foresight and foresight with achievement'.[60] If we would balance intellectual activity and the development of character, therefore, we need to adopt 'the way of literary culture, the way of scientific culture, the way of technical culture'.[61] But if we follow one way to the exclusion of the others, then intellectual activity will suffer, and character will be undermined. 'The problem of education is to retain the dominant emphasis, whether literary, scientific, or technical, and without loss of co-ordination to infuse into each way of education something of the other two.'[62]

This approach to education would have met with the whole-hearted approval of Gandhi, for whom the spinning-wheel was a symbol of self-reliance, and handicrafts an essential prerequisite of the national educational curriculum. He would have approved also of Whitehead's telling injunction that nothing indicated the failure of education more than 'inert ideas' or 'mental dry rot'.[63]

When Whitehead speaks of self-development as 'the valuable aspect of intellectual development'[64] he is not be far removed from Plato's educational aim to cultivate the soul, or from Gandhi's desire to nurture the whole man, body, mind and spirit; to develop character; and to know the *Ātman*, or the self within. True the *Atman* has a different connotation in Gandhi's philosophy, and that knowing the self within has religious and philosophical implication which are not to be found in Whitehead's philosophy. Yet it is significant that the latter views the essence of education as being religious, and that he sees the purpose of religious education as inculcating duty and reverence.'Duty arises from our potential control over the course of events...And the foundation of reverence is this perception, that the present holds within itself the complete sum of existence, backwards and forwards, that whole amplitude of time, which is eternity.'[65] Gandhi's thoughts on religious education, which we dealt with in an earlier chapter, are not dissimilar to those of Whitehead, except that the latter sees eternity in the realm of becoming, while Gandhi, like Plato, draws a distinction between the realm of being and the realm of becoming.

From the comparisons we have endeavoured to draw between Gandhi's philosophy of education and the theories of education we have enumerated, we can conclude that he need not have been so reluctant to express his views on the subject. He may not have been an educationist in the generally accepted sense of the term, and he was certainly no expert in educational theory, but the views he expressed on the type of education his country needed command respect, and are worthy of consideration and comment. It may be possible to accuse him of being presumptuous in the extreme in seeking to lecture educational experts on the purpose of education, since he lacked any kind of academic distinction or expertise in the subject. Yet his quest for Truth, his firm belief in the unity of existence, and his concern for *sarvodaya*, prompted him to overcome his reluctance and fears, and to express his views in a forthright fashion. That he did so has enabled us to examine the avant garde nature of some of his beliefs, and to draw comparisons with the reformers of the Hindu tradition. The similarity of his views with those of Western commentators on education also, has helped to illuminate the contemporary nature of his philosophy of education.

Notes

1. Plato, *The Laws*, translated by Trevor J. Saunders, Penguin Books, Harmandsworth 1970, p. 644. Quoted in Robert R. Rusk and James Scotland, *Doctrines of the Great Educators*, Macmillan, Fifth Edition, London, 1979, p. 11
2. *Crito*, p. 45. See *Plato Works*, translated by Benjamin Jowett, Oxford University Press, 1875. See Rusk and Scotland, *op. cit.* p. 11
3. *Crito*, p. 50. See *Works*
4. *Protagoras*, pp. 325–6. See *Works*. See Rusk and Scotland, *op. cit.* p. 12
5. Jean-Jacques Rousseau, *Emile*, Everyman Edition, translated by Barbara Foxley, Dent, London 1911, p. 8. See Rusk and Scotland, *op. cit.* p. 13
6. *Plato, The Republic*, p. 415. translated by A.D. Lindsay, J.M. Dent, London, 1948.
7. *Politics*, vii, p. 17. See Robin Barrow, *Plato, Utilitarianism and Education*, Routledge & Kegan Paul, London, 1975, p.151
8. *The Republic*, pp. 376, 410
9. Ibid., p. 378
10. Ibid., p. 386
11. Ibid., pp. 386–8
12. Ibid., p. 389
13. Ibid., p. 401
14. Ibid., p. 401
15. *Politics*, vii,17
16. *The Republic*, p. 411
17. *The Laws*, p. 795, cf. pp. 814–16
18. *The Republic*, p. 411
19. Ibid., pp. 490, 487
20. Ibid., p. 521
21. Ibid., p. 518
22. Ibid., p. 527
23. Ibid.
24. Ibid., p. 533

25. Ibid., p. 534
26. Ibid., pp. 451–7
27. *The Laws*, pp. 643–4
28. Ibid., p. 643
29. A.N. Whitehead, *The Aims of Education*, William and Norgate, London, 1929, p. 71, Benn, London, 1962
30. Paul Tillich, *Theology of Education*, mss. delivered at St. Paul's School, Concord, New Hampshire, on 13 October 1956, pp. 1–8
31. Ibid., p. 4
32. *The Collected Works of Mahatma Gandhi*, Second Revised Edition, Ministry of Information and Broadcasting, Government of India, New Delhi, (hereafter, CWMG), Vol. 49, pp. 50–51
33. M. Montessori, *The Secret of Childhood*, translated and edited by Barbara B. Carter, Longmans, London, 1936, pp. 69, 137
34. CWMG, Vol. 45, p. 63
35. Ibid., Vol. 60, pp. 42–3
36. M. Montessori, *The Advanced Montessori Method*, translated by Florence Simmonds and Lily Hutchinson, William Heinmannn, London, 1917, Vol. 1, pp. 19–22
37. M. Montessori, *The Absorbent Mind*, Theosophical Press, Wheaton Illinois 1964, p. 140
38. Paula P. Lillard, *Montessori: A Modern Approach*, Schocken Books, New York, 1972, p. 120
39. M. Montessori, *The Montessori Method*, translated by Anne E. George, William Heinmann, London, 1912, p. 104
40. Ibid., p. 261
41. CWMG, Vol. 69, pp. 370–77
42. M.K. Gandhi, *All Men are Brothers*, edited by Krishna Kripalani, UNESCO, Paris, 1958, 1969, p. 151
43. CWMG, Vol. 21, p. 39
44. Ibid.
45. *Aims of Education*, Williams and Norgate, London, 1929, Benn, London, 1962, p. 77. Cf. A.N. Whitehead, *An Anthology*, selected by F.S.C. Northrop & Mason W. Gross, Cambridge University Press, Cambridge, 1953, p. 107
46. *An Anthology*, p. 103
47. Ibid., p. 92
48. Ibid., p. 91
49. Ibid., pp. 90–91
50. Ibid., p. 87
51. Ibid., p. 88
52. Ibid., p. 92
53. *Aims of Education*, 75. Cf. *An Anthology*, p. 105

54. Ibid., pp. 68–9. Cf. *An Anthology*, pp. 101–2, 111
55. Ibid., pp. 1–2. Cf. *An Anthology*, p. 87
56. *An Anthology*, p. 104
57. Ibid., p. 105
58. Ibid., p. 106
59. Ibid., p. 107
60. Ibid., pp. 110–11
61. Ibid., p. 111
62. Ibid.
63. Ibid., pp. 87–8
64. Ibid., p. 87
65. Ibid., p. 100

chapter eight

Conclusion

I have endeavoured to show that an understanding of what Gandhi means by Truth is an essential precondition for any assessment of his philosophy as a whole, and of his philosophy of education in particular. His experiments with truth determine every aspect of his teaching, and it is especially true of his view of education. We have seen that as a self-professed Advaitin he accepts that knowing the *Ātman* is akin to knowing the nature of Ultimate Reality, *Brahman*. He equates Reality, *Sat*, with Truth, *Satya*, since for him nothing exists except Truth, for where Truth is, there also is Reality. We have examined the similarity of his views with the classical Advaitin views of Sankara, and with the neo-Vedāntic views of Vivekananda, and we have shown that although he is closer to the views of the latter, he is nevertheless justified in claiming to believe in *Advaita*.[1] His views concerning the nature of the Self, *Ātman*, and its relation to Truth, *Satya*, is derived from the religious tradition in which he was nurtured. The whole purpose of life, in his view, is to know the Self: this also is the goal of true education, by means of which we come to know the *Ātman* and the nature of Truth.[2] Similar views are expressed by Teresa of Avila when she maintains that our knowledge of God is linked to self-understanding, and that knowing the self is rooted in the religious and cultural traditions in which we were nurtured.[3] Education for Gandhi, as we have seen, requires breadth in the sense of mental and physical development in order to be successful, but should it lack depth in the sense of understanding the nature of the Self, then it cannot be regarded as true education. It is one thing to cultivate the mind and the body: it is another thing to nurture the soul.

Hence music, as the language of the soul, is necessary for the cultivation of the spirit and knowledge of Truth, since it leads man to a vision of God. The divine nature of music is such that when life is permeated with it, man is united with God.[4] It is the essential component of true education because it contributes to self-realization, the realization of Truth, or God, and an understanding of the nature of Ultimate Reality.

To know the true nature of the Self, however, is to realize at the same time the unitary nature of existence. We may have many bodies, but there is one soul, and the manifold is simply a manifestation of the one.[5] All men are brothers because they share the same *Ātman* and are bound together in the bond of Truth. Hence the need for us to accept responsibility for our fellow-men no matter how lowly and deprived they may be. *Sarvodaya* is the logical consequence of self-realization, and the realization of the unitary nature of existence. In the field of education accepting responsibility for the less fortunate members of Hindu society involves providing them with the means of improving their lot. Harijans and women, who have hitherto been ignored and neglected, need to be uplifted, and given the kind of education that would enable them to enrich the quality of their lives, and radically change their social status. Gandhi's educational programme has the condition of these unfortunate members of Indian society very clearly in mind. We have shown that he considers it to be necessary for education to be open to all and not confined to the elite, or the more fortunate members of Hindu society. In his view it is the basic right of all to be uplifted, for *sarvodaya* is the inescapable corollary of self-realization.

The needs of adults and children are equally provided for in Gandhi's constructive programme of education. Its primary aim, as we have endeavoured to show, is the elimination of illiteracy. This could not be effected without a radical overhaul of the entire educational programme of the country, and the creation of an alternative system that would cater for the masses. At the same time as providing training in literacy and numeracy, however, the basic educational programme he envisages stresses the importance of the creative skills involved in handicrafts.[6] Acquiring these creative skills in the early years of primary education is not unrelated to what he has to say about the dignity of labour, and the symbolic significance of the spinning-wheel. The latter is above all a symbol of self-respect, self-reliance, and economic self-sufficiency. The concepts of *swadeshī* and *khadī*, derive from his belief in the importance of self-respect and self-reliance, and illustrate his desire to make his constructive programme of education self-sufficient. This attitude would have met with the approval of Whitehead for whom education had to combine liberal, scientific, and technical approaches at all levels in order to preserve the imaginative acquisition of knowledge.[7] Like Whitehead, Gandhi draws no distinction between intellectual and vocational training and this applies as much to higher education as to education at the primary level. Universities as well as schools could benefit from the combination of what Whitehead refers to as the liberal, scientific and technical approaches.

Society as a whole could benefit from Gandhi's alternative system of education. His desire to encourage self-respect, and self-reliance, as we have shown, involves creating an awareness of the cultural heritage of the nation. There could be no sense of self-identity without an awareness of one's roots in a community that shared the same cultural traditions. The alien system of education that had been imposed on the nation undermined those traditions. Hence his insistence that the hypnotic spell of the English language be removed.[8] The imposition of a foreign language as the medium of instruction in schools and colleges, to the exclusion of the indigenous languages, meant that an intellectual and moral injury was being inflicted on the Indian nation by undermining its literary foundations and ignoring its cultural heritage. It was a grievous blow to self-identity, and to the national identity of the Indian people.[9] The importance of knowing the self is that it constitutes the basis of self-reliance, and is the starting point of the quest for self-rule and *swarāj*. There could be no *swarāj* without self-reliance and an awareness of one's own identity.

The importance of religion in the quest for self-realization and self-identity cannot be over-estimated, because for Gandhi, as we have seen, the main purpose of true education is the nurture of the soul. This is in accord with the views of Plato, for whom the development of character and the cultivation of the spirit are paramount, and corresponds to Whitehead's belief that the essence of education is that it be religious.[10] We have shown that Gandhi's indebtedness to the religious tradition in which he was nurtured enabled him to describe himself as an Advaitin, and he was justified in so doing because of the similarity of his views with those of Sankara and Vivekananda. It is as a self-professed Advaitin that he is able to equate knowing the Self, the *Ātman*, with knowing God, or Truth, *Satya*, and knowing the true nature of Reality,

Sat. Hence his belief that education has to be ethically and religiously oriented, and that without religion it is fruitless. The study of religion is essential in any programme of true education, yet this does not imply that secular education can be ignored: both are necessary in a balanced educational programme.

The type of religious studies he favours, however, is not the narrow, dogmatic, exclusivist kind that would elevate a particular religion to a position of superiority over all others. He supports rather, as we have seen, the open-ended approach that would examine the tenets of faiths other than one's own: the ethical teachings of all religions, and the beliefs and doctrines of the great religions of the world in a spirit of reverence and tolerance. He is favourably disposed to what would be referred to today as religious pluralism, since nothing could give greater personal, spiritual assurance, or provide a better appreciation of one's own religion.[11] In this respect he is in accord with the open-ended, pluralistic, dialogical approach to religious studies favoured by John Hick, for whom God is at work in the whole religious life of mankind; Raimundo Panikkar, for whom faith in the truth is paramount; and Ninian Smart for whom the narrow, restricted, dogmatic approach to religious studies is inadequate. It could be argued, however, that Gandhi's avant garde approach to the study of religion may have been one of the reasons why he had not been able to convince many people of the correctness of his views on education.[12]

Yet his educational philosophy echoes the teaching of many Hindu reformers. He is in accord with the views of Rammohan Roy in seeking to broaden the intellectual horizons of his fellow-countrymen. Roy sought to provide them with a more liberal form of education embracing the natural sciences, rather than seeking to acquire a mastery of Sanskrit.[13] Gandhi was concerned with imparting valuable knowledge through the use of the indigenous languages as the medium of instruction in education, rather than seeking in the first instance to acquire a mastery of English. He is in agreement with Dayananda Sarasvati also in his support of the vernacular, and with the general thrust of his argument that self-identity and national identity were endangered when native languages were neglected.[14] His theory of education, as we have shown, echoes also the teachings of Vivekananda, who fervently believed that the mass of ordinary people in India should be educated in order that their eyes might be opened to the possibilities that existed in the world around them, and that they might become fully human, or *develop their lost individuality*.[15] Both were concerned with *sarvodaya*, since both sought to improve the lot of ordinary people by providing them with educational opportunities similar to those available to the higher castes of Indian society.

Tilak's views are reflected in Gandhi's philosophy, especially in respect of religious studies and the compulsory study of English in schools. Tilak deplored the latter believing that it should be abolished, and with regard to the former, he favoured an open and tolerant approach involving the study of religions other than Hinduism. They were in agreement also in the belief that education and *swarāj* went hand in hand. As descendants of Akbar and Ashoka, Tilak believed that the Indian people were perfectly capable of self-government, and like Gandhi was of the view that education was the key to enabling them to manage their own affairs.[16]

Unlike Tilak, who was of the view that a woman's place is in the home, Gokhale believed that the only way to emancipate women from their bondage to a demeaning way of life was to provide them with educational opportunities. In this respect he was at one with Gandhi for whom education was the key to a better way of life for these more unfortunate members of Indian society. They agreed on the need for primary education for the masses in order that illiteracy might be eliminated, and the foundations of a more just and equitable society be laid.[17]

The rural nature of the setting for Rabindranath Tagore's Vishva Bharati University at Shantiniketan reflects his views on the relation that he conceived exists between God, man and nature, for the same power that created the universe enlightens man's consciousness. The whole purpose of life is to realize the presence of the divine in the soul, and the ultimate goal of education is to effect this realization. Tagore's philosophy concurs with Gandhi's belief that no distinction can be drawn between *Ātman* and *Brahman*, the essence of the universe, and that the goal of true education is the realization of the Self and the nature of Truth.[18] Again both are in agreement about the importance of the mother tongue as the medium of instruction in education, and the need for the harmonious development of the whole man, body, mind, and spirit.[19]

Vinoba Bhave, as an ardent disciple, reflects the teaching of Gandhi in a variety of ways. Self-government meant educating people so that they could manage their own affairs, and the concept of *Nai Talim*, new education, meant educating people for life in such a way that work and learning could be combined.[20] He is in agreement with Gandhi when he refers to religious studies as being concerned with the cultivation of sound character, and when he recognizes that the soul is other than the body.[21] Again his stress on the importance of knowing the self echoes much of what Gandhi has to say about the *Ātman-Brahman* identity.[22]

Radhakrishnan's belief that the purpose of education is self-knowledge,[23] and its ultimate aim the preservation of the integrity of man's soul,[24] is also in accord with Gandhi's view that the goal of education is to know the Self, and true education the recognition that there can be no distinction between the Self, *Ātman*, and Truth, *Satya*. Clearly Gandhi is at one with the views of both Bhave and Radhakrishnan, and in many respects he upholds the tradition of the Hindu reformers.

What is most significant about Gandhi's philosophy of education, however, is the way in which it reflects the teaching of other philosophers, theologians, and educationists. Plato favoured the type of education that led to the cultivation of the soul. He was concerned with high standards of intellectual integrity and morality for the gold and silver classes in particular, but in addition sought the welfare and happiness of all, in the same way as Gandhi sought the uplift of all.[25] For Plato education did not consist in the accumulation of factual knowledge, but rather the contemplation of real existence: contemplation of the transcendental rather than the empirical, the realm of being rather than the realm of becoming.[26] For Gandhi too, the goal of education is to know the Self; recognize the identity of *Ātman-Brahman;* develop the whole man, body mind and spirit; and understand the meaning of the quest for Truth.[27] They differ in their attitude to what Plato calls the artisans, and Gandhi refers to as the unfortunate members of society, but on the question of the primary purpose of education they would seem to be in accord.

As we have noted Tillich sought to harmonize three main aims of education, namely, the technical, humanistic, and inductive, which stress the acquisition of skills, the promotion of intellectual discipline, and the preservation of social traditions respectively. Concentration on one of these aims to the exclusion of the other two led to difficulties, whereas the harmonization of all three meant that creative skills, intellectual disciplines and social traditions were enhanced and preserved.[28] Gandhi proposed similar goals when he stressed the importance of crafts in education, the need for the use of the vernacular as the medium of instruction so that participants were not separated from their roots in society, and the significance of knowing the true nature of the Self. His programme of constructive, religious, and what he calls true education, incorporates the technical, humanistic, and inductive aims of education which Tillich sought to harmonize.

Gandhi's desire to combine the creativity of crafts and intellectual skills[29] indicates how much he was in accord with the Montessori method of teaching, which he commends for its Platonic combination of music and bodily exercises, and its stress on the importance of a proper environment for teaching.[30] In this respect Montessori echoes Tagore's beliefs which led him to establish his University in the rural setting of Shantiniketan. Tagore's goal was the cultivation of the whole man, the liberation of the human spirit, and the emancipation of the soul. This is very much in line with Gandhi's view that it is possible to imbibe culture as much from the environment as from the manner in which it is imparted, and that the ultimate goal of education is the cultivation of character.[31]

Gandhi's wholehearted approval of vocational training as an essential element in education indicates, as we have seen, that he was in agreement with the educational aims of Whitehead, for whom no curriculum could be considered complete without the inclusion of technical subjects.[32] Whitehead disapproved of the negative aspect of Plato's educational philosophy as the result of which the artisans fared badly in comparison with the guardians and auxiliaries. On the other hand he approved of the positive aspect of Plato's philosophy whereby art was encouraged, and human dignity defended against the forces of materialism that tended to undermine it.[33] In this respect he is in agreement with Gandhi, for whom dignity and virtue are to the forefront of his educational programme as his emphasis on *sarvodaya* shows. They are united also in their assessment that true education is not the acquisition of inert ideas but the art of applying ideas to practical issues.[34] Both favoured the active rather than the passive approach to education, or the passive reception of the ideas of others.[35] Hence, for Whitehead, technical education with its emphasis on manual skills, was as important as scientific knowledge and aesthetic appreciation. This approach is in accord with the approach of Gandhi for whom crafts and vocational training were the essential prerequisites of his alternative system of education. Again Whitehead stresses self-development as a valuable aspect of intellectual development, while Plato speaks of the need to cultivate the soul, and

Gandhi refers to the importance of seeking to nurture the whole man, body, mind and spirit; to develop character; and to know the Self. Knowing the *Ātman*, *however*, has religious and philosophical connotations which are not present in Whitehead's philosophy, yet it is significant that the latter sees the essence of education as being religious.[36]

What we have had to say about Gandhi's philosophy of education leads us to reaffirm the view that he was certainly avant garde in his approach, and that some of his views have a contemporary ring. That he should have been reluctant to express his views is understandable, but given his conformity to the views of other Hindu reformers, and the parallels that have been drawn with other philosophers and educationists, it can be argued that it was hardly necessary for him to be so fearful about expressing his views. He asks questions concerning the aim and purpose of education that are at the forefront of the minds of many philosophers, and the conclusions he arrives at are not dissimilar to those of other educationists. That he was concerned with breadth of education is evidenced by his desire to extend educational opportunities to all, and his plea for a balanced educational programme involving creative skills as well as intellectual pursuits. That he was concerned with depth of education is evidenced by his desire to seek the cultivation of the spirit in addition to the development of the body and the mind. For him character-building, involving moral and ethical teaching, was an essential aspect of education. Religious studies was as important as secular instruction in a programme of education designed to develop the whole man, body, mind and spirit. We conclude that his Platonic spirit, his Tillichian approach, his Montessorian methodology, and his Whiteheadian emphasis, places him in the vanguard of those who would propound an acceptable philosophy of education.

Notes

1. N.K. Bose, *Selections from Gandhi*, Navajivan Trust, Ahmedabad, 1948, p. 92

2. *The Collected Works of Mahatma Gandhi* (hereafter, CWMG), Second Revised Edition, Ministry of Information and Broadcasting, Government of India, New Delhi, 1969–, Vol. 50, p. 182

3. See *The Life of Teresa of Jesus: the Autobiography of St. Teresa of Avila*, translated and edited by E. Allison Peers from the critical edition of

P. Silverio de Santa Teresa, Image Books, New York: Garden City 1960; *Interior Castle*, Doubleday, New York, 1989; *Autobiography of St. Teresa of Avila*, Doubleday, New York, 1991

4. CWMG, Vol. 37, pp. 2–3
5. Louis Fischer, Editor, *The Essential Gandhi*, Vintage Books, New York, 1962, p. 229
6. CWMG, Vol. 66, p. 169
7. A.N. Whitehead, *An Anthology*, selected by F.S.C. Northrop & Mason W. Gross, Cambridge University Press, Cambridge, 1953, p. 130
8. CWMG, Vol. 41, pp. 173–5
9. Ibid., Vol. 66, p. 194
10. A.N. Whitehead, *An Anthology*, p. 100
11. CWMG, Vol. 37, pp. 254–5
12. Ibid., Vol. 54, p. 423
13. *English Works of Raja Rammohun Roy*, edited by Dr Kalidas Nag and Debajyoti Burman, Sadaran Brahma Samaj, Calcutta, 1945-51, Part IV, 1946, pp. 105–8
14. *Autobiography of Dayananda Sarasvati*, edited by K.C. Yadav, Second Revised Edition, Manohar Publications, New Delhi, 1978, p. 70
15. *The Complete Works of Swami Vivekananda*, Vols. I-VIII, Advaita Ashram, Calcutta, 1970, Vol IV, pp. 362–3
16. *Bal Gangadhar Tilak. His Writings and Speeches*, Third Edition, Ganesh and Co., Madras 1922, pp. 254–5, 117–8
17. *Speeches of Gopal Krishna Gokhale*, Third Edition, G.A. Natesan and Co., Madras 1920, pp. 608, 882–3; *The Selected Works of Mahatma Gandhi*, edited by Shriman Narayan, Navajivan Trust, Ahmedabad, 1968, pp. 507, 512
18. Rabindranath Tagore, *Towards Universal Man*, Asia Publishing House, Bombay, 1961, p. 75; *Selections from Gandhi*, p. 288
19. Ibid., pp. 43–6
20. Vinoba Bhave, *Thoughts on Education*, Akhil Bharat Sarva Seva Sangh, Rajghat, Kashi, Varanasi, 1959, p. 234
21. Ibid., p. 117
22. Ibid., p. 252
23. Sarvepalli Radhakrishnan, *Education, Politics and War*, International Book Service, Poona, 1944, p. 101
24. Ibid., p. 88
25. *Plato, The Republic*, translated by A.D. Lindsay, J.M. Dent, London, 1948, p. 376, p. 410
26. Ibid., p. 521, p. 518
27. CWMG, Vol. 50, p. 182, 185; Vol. 73, p. 235
28. Paul Tillich, *Theology of Education*, mss. delivered at St. Paul's School, Concord, New Hampshire, on October 13, 1956, pp. 1–8
29. CWMG, Vol. 69, pp. 370–77

30. M. Montessori, *The Secret of Childhood*, translated and edited by Barbara B. Carter, Longmans, London, 1936, 69, p. 137
31. CWMG, Vol. 45, p. 63
32. *Aims of Education*, Williams and Norgate, London 1929, Benn, London 1962, p. 77. Cf. A.N. Whitehead, *An Anthology*, p. 107
33. *An Anthology*, p. 103
34. Ibid., pp. 90–1
35. Ibid., p. 104
36. Ibid., p. 100

Bibliography

Autobiography of St. Teresa of Àvila, Doubleday, New York, 1991

Bal Gangadhar Tilak. His Writings and Speeches, Third Edition, Ganesh and Co., Madras, 1922

Barrow, Robin, *Plato, Utilitarianism and Education*, Routledge & Kegan Paul, London, 1975

Barth, Karl, *Church Dogmatics*, Vol. I, Parts 1 & 2, G.W. Bromiley and T.F. Torrance, (eds), T. and T. Clark, Edinburgh, 1956

Bhave, Vinoba, *Democratic Values and the Practice of Citizenship, Selections from the Addresses of Vinoba Bhave 1951–1968*, (trans.) Marjorie Sykes, Sarva Seva Sangh Prakashan, Kashi, Rajghat, Varanasi, 1962

————, *Thoughts on Education*, Akhil Bharat Sarva Seva Sangh, Rajghat, Kashi, Varanasi, 1959

Bose, N.K., *Selections from Gandhi*, Navajivan Trust, Ahmedabad, 1948, 1972

Brunner, Emil, *Revelation and Reason*, (trans.) Olive Wyon, SCM Press, London, 1947

Buber, Martin, *I and Thou*, (trans.) Ronald Gregor Smith. T. & T. Clark, Edinburgh, 1937, 1953

Chatterjee, Margaret, *Gandhi's Religious Thought*, Macmillan, London, 1983

Complete Works of Vivekananda The, Vols. I-VIII, Advaita Ashrama, Calcutta, 1970

Conger, George P., 'Radhakrishnan's World', *The Philosophy of Sarvepalli Radhakrishnan*, Paul Arthur Schilpp, (ed.), Motilal Banarsidass, Delhi, 1992

Donaldson, Margaret, *Children's Minds*, Collins, Glasgow, 1978, 1981

Edwards, Owen, *Clych Atgof: Penodau yn hanes fy Addysg*, Cwmni Cyhoeddwyr Cymreig, Caernarfon, 1906

Fischer, Louis, (ed.), *The Essential Gandhi*, New York, Vintage Books, 1962

Fischer, Louis, *The Life of Mahatma Gandhi*, HarperCollins, London, 1997

Gandhi, M.K., *All Men are Brothers*, Krishna Kripalani, (ed.), UNESCO, Paris, 1958, 1969

———, *An Autobiography*, translated from Gujarati by Mahadev Desai, Jonathan Cape, London, 1972

———, *In Search of the Supreme*, Navajivan Trust, Ahmedabad, 1931

———, *Truth is God*, Navajivan Trust, Ahmedabad, 1955

Gutierrez, Gustavo, *A Theology of Liberation*, SCM Press, London, 1974

Hick, John, 'Jesus and the World Religions', *The Myth of God Incarnate*, John Hick, (ed.), SCM Press, London, 1977

———, *God and the Universe of Faiths*, Collins, Glasgow, 1977

———, *God Has Many Names*, Macmillan, London, 1980

Hiryanna, M., *Outlines of Indian Philosophy*, George Allen and Unwin, Bombay, 1973

Iyer, Raghavan, *The Moral and Political Writings of Mahatma Gandhi*, Clarendon Press, Oxford 1987

Jenkins, Islwyn, *Idris Davies of Rhymney*, Gomer Press, Llandysul, 1986

Kalidas, Nag, and Debajyoti Burman, (eds), *English Works of Raja Rammohun Roy*, Sadaran Brahma Samaj, Calcutta, 1945-51

Koestler, Arthur, 'The Yogi and the Commissar', *New York Times Magazine*, October, 1969

Lillard, Paula P., *Montessori: A Modern Approach*, Schocken Books, New York, 1972

Montessori, M., *The Absorbent Mind*, Wheaton Illinois, Theosophical Press, 1964

———, *The Montessori Method*, translated by Anne E. George, William Heinmann, London, 1912

———, *The Secret of Childhood*, translated and edited by Barbara B. Carter, Longmans, London, 1936.

Madhavananda, Swami, (ed.), *Vivekachudamani of Sri Sankaracharya*, Advaita Ashrama, Calcutta, 1970

Montessori, *The Advanced Montessori Method*, (trans.) Florence Simmonds and Lily Hutchinson, William Heinmann, London, 1917

Otto, Rudolf, *Mysticism East and West*, Macmillan, New York, 1972

Panikkar, Raimundo, *The Intra-Religious Dialogue*, Paulist Press, New York, 1978

Peers, E. Allison, (trans. and ed.), from the critical edition of P. Silverio de Santa Teresa, Garden City, *The Life of Teresa of Jesus: The Aubotiography of St. Teresa of Avila*, Image Books, New York, 1960.

Peters, R.S., (ed.), *The Philosophy of Education*, Oxford University Press, Oxford, 1973.

Plato, *The Laws*, (trans.) Trevor J. Saunders, Penguin Books, Harmandsworth, 1970

———, *The Republic*, (trans.) A.D. Lindsay, J.M. Dent, London, 1948

———, *Works*, (trans.) Benjamin Jowett, Oxford University Press, Oxford, 1875

Radhakrishnan, Sarvepalli, *Education, Politics and War*, International Book Service, Poona, 1944

———, *Indian Religions*, Vision Books, New Delhi, 1979

———, *Kalki or the Future of Civilisation*, Kegan and Paul, London, 1929

———, *The Hindu View of Life*, George Allen and Unwin, London, 1964

Richards, Glyn, (ed.), *A Source Book of Modern Hinduism*, Curzon Press, London and Dublin, 1985

———, *Studies in Religion*, Macmillan, London, 1995

———, *The Philosophy of Gandhi*, Curzon Press, London and Dublin, 1982

———, *Towards a Theology of Religions*, Routledge, London and New York, 1989

Rousseau, Jean-Jacques, *Emile*, Everyman Edition, (trans.) Barbara Foxley, Dent, London, 1911

Rusk, Robert R., and James Scotland, *Doctrines of the Great Educators*, Fifth Edition, Macmillan, London, 1979

Saxena, S. K., 'The fabric of self-suffering in Gandhi', *Religious Studies*, XII, 2, Cambridge University Press, Cambridge, 1976

Shriman, Narayan, (ed.), *The Selected Works of Mahatma Gandhi*, Navajivan trust, Ahmedabad, 1968, Vols. I-VI.

Smart, Ninian, *Secular Education and the Logic of Religion*, Heslington Lectures, University of York, 1966, Faber and Faber, London, 1968

Smart, J.J.C., and Bernard Williams, *Utilitarianism For and Against*, Cambridge, 1973

Speeches of Gopal Krishna Gokhale, Third Edition, G.A. Natesan and Co., Madras, 1920

Sutherland, Stewart, *The Price of Ignorance*, Hume Occasional Paper No. 47, The David Hume Institute, Edinburgh, 1995

Tagore, Rabindranath, *Personality: Lectures Delivered in America*, Macmillan, London, 1921

———, *Towards Universal Man*, Asia Publishing House, Bombay, 1961

Teresa of Avila, *Interior Castle*, Doubleday, New York, 1989

The Collected Works of Mahatma Gandhi, Second Revised Edition, Ministry of Information and Broadcasting, Government of India, New Delhi, 1969–, Vols. 1–77

Thibaut, George, (ed.), *The Vedanta Sutras of Badarayana with the Commentary by Sankara*, Dover, New York, 1962.

Thomas, C. Owen, (ed.), *Attitudes Towards Other Religions*, Harper and Row, New York, 1969

Tillich, Paul, *Theology of Education*. Mss. delivered at St. Paul's School, Concord, New Hampshire, 13 October 1956

———, *Ultimate Concern: Tillich in Dialogue*, Harper and Row, New York, 1965

Troeltsch, Ernst, 'The Place of Christianity Among the World Religions', *Christian Thought: Its History and Application*, Meridian Books, New York, University of London Press, London, 1957

Troeltsch, Ernest, *The Aboluteness of Christianity and the History of Religions*, S.C.M. Press, London, 1972

Whitehead, A.N., *Adventure of Ideas*, Cambridge University Press, Cambridge, 1939

————, *An Anthology*, selected by F.S.C. Northrop & Mason W. Gross, Cambridge University Press, Cambridge, 1953

————, *The Aims of Education*, William and Norgate, London, 1929; Benn, London, 1962

Winch, Peter, 'Understanding a Primitive Society', *Religion and Understanding*, edited by D.Z. Phillips, Blackwell, Oxford, 1967

Wordsworth, William, *Poetical Works*, Thomas Hutchinson, (ed.), Oxford University Press, Oxford, 1973

Yadav, K.V., (ed.), *Autobiography of Dayananda Sarasvati*, Second Revised Edition, Manohar Publications, New Delhi, 1978

Glossary

Advaita Vedānta	:	philosophical school of non-dualism
adhyasā	:	illegitimate transference
ahiṁsā	:	non-violence
anekāntavāda	:	non-unitary nature of reality; a view maintaining the manyness, or many-aspectness, of reality
Ātman	:	Self within; soul; essence of life
avidyā	:	ignorance
Brahman	:	Ultimate Reality; Being itself; Ground of Being
Brahmins	:	Members of the highest caste
Daridrānāryan	:	God of the poor
dharma	:	duty; law
Dvaita	:	dualism; philosophical system expounded by Madhva in the twelfth century
gramrāj	:	village government
Harijans	:	children of God
Īśvara	:	God; Lord
jivan mukta	:	the liberated soul
jñāna	:	knowledge
karma	:	action
khadi	:	home-spun cloth
Kṣatriyas	:	Members of the warrior caste
lilā	:	sport
lok-niti	:	government of the people, and by the people
māyā	:	illusion
mokṣa	:	liberation
Nai Talim	:	new education, or education for life
nirguṇa	:	without qualities

prakṛti	:	nature
purdah	:	pertaining to the seclusion of women
ṛta	:	cosmic moral law
Saccidānanda	:	Reality, Knowledge, Bliss: related to Truth and Brahman
śakti	:	power
Sankara	:	Expounder of the Advaita Vedānta philosophical system in the eighth century
samādhi	:	state of complete meditation; concentrated thought
saṁsāra	:	bondage of birth, death and rebirth; empirical existence
sarvodaya	:	welfare of all; universal well-being
Sat	:	Reality; Being
Satya	:	Truth
satyāgraha	:	holding fast to truth; truth force
Śūdras	:	Members of the lower caste
swadeshī	:	self-reliance
swarāj	:	self-rule
Vaiśyas	:	Members of the artisan caste
varṇāśramadharma	:	duties pertaining to one's caste or social status
vidyapith	:	a seat of learning
Viśiṣṭādvaita	:	modified non-dualism; non-dualism with distinctions; philosphical system expounded by Ramanuja in the tenth century
vivartavāda	:	Sankara's view that the world is the phenomenal appearance of Brahman
yoga	:	discipline

Index